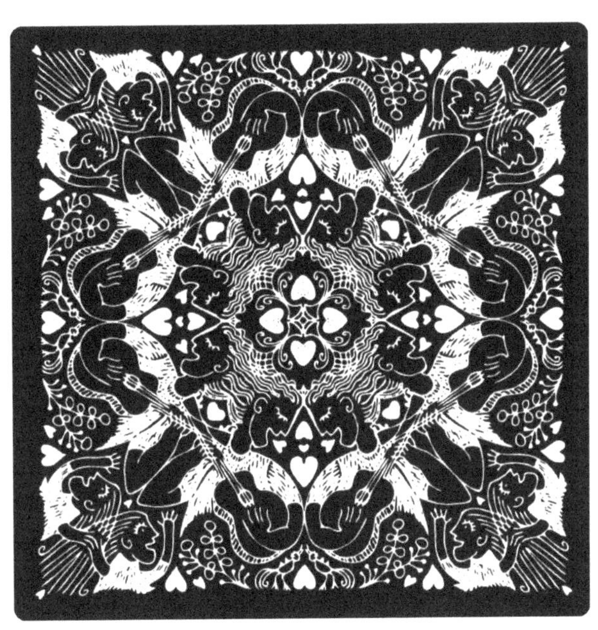

The Unexpected Stories

In 2014, I did a series of many drawings for coloring books. Early in 2021, I had a dream where I took them and printed them on tiles.

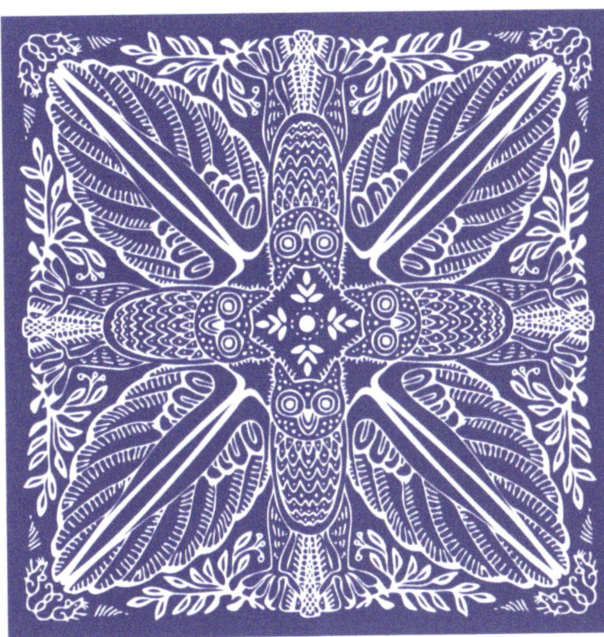

So I chose one of those designs and got it made into a tile - and loved it so much I was lit on fire with idea after idea. This book is the result of some of that stream of creation.

These images are great for so many uses besides tiles - more about that in the next section.

All these images are vectorized, so they can be scaled for tiny reproduction all the way up to giant wall-sized displays.

The images shown in the book are done in black and white so you can see details well. It is really easy to shift them to any color you desire.

Enquiries:
Angela Treat Lyon
530.809.7900
Lyon@AngelaTreatLyon.com
UnexpectedStoryArt.com

Unexpected Stories

Collections including silly critters, sports, love, food, and music

Angela Treat Lyon

ISBN: 978-0-578-92370-3

Book cover, formatting, design, production & publication
by Angela Treat Lyon

Published and printed in the United States

Published by
Out Front Productions
Chico, California

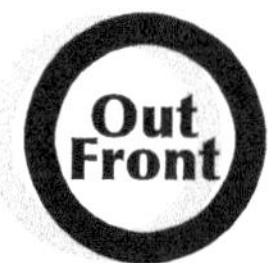

Unexpected Stories

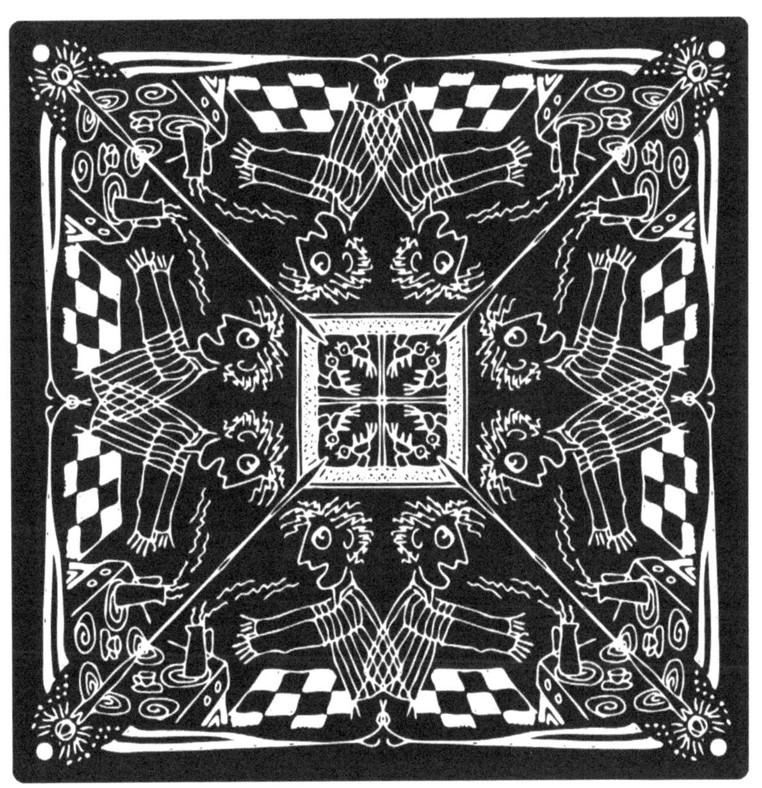

Angela Treat Lyon

How to 'read' the story images

If you look casually at any of these designs, they seem to look like geometric snow-flakey kinds of designs. But when you get up close, all of a sudden... hey wait a minute! There's a guy in there - and cakes, and dogs, and kitties, and birdies.... Each design is a surprise. That's why I call them 'unexpected.'

I like it that way. The images are so much more interesting than, say, a scene of a nice farm, or a guy on a boat, or (yawn) most other mundane pictures or geometric designs you can find in old tiles.

Due to the complexity of detail, though, some people don't see the scenes.

So, I made a few images that show you *how to look* at each one so you can see who and what is in each image.

Designs can be based on multiples of 4, 6 and 8. Most of them are 4-based because that gives me more room to draw.

STEP ONE: Look at the overall image. You should be able to count the segments pretty easily. Find the major points first. This image here has 6 main segments.

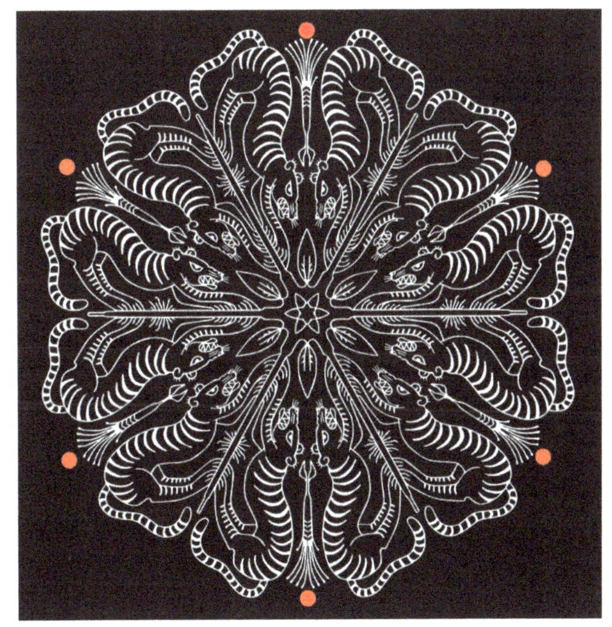

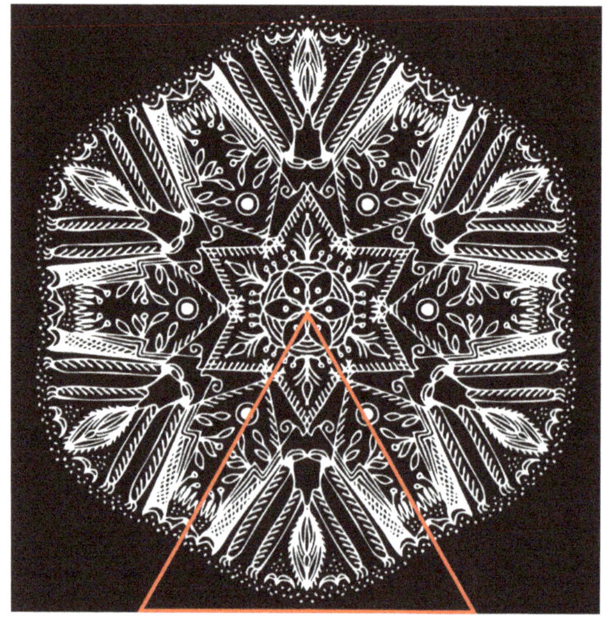

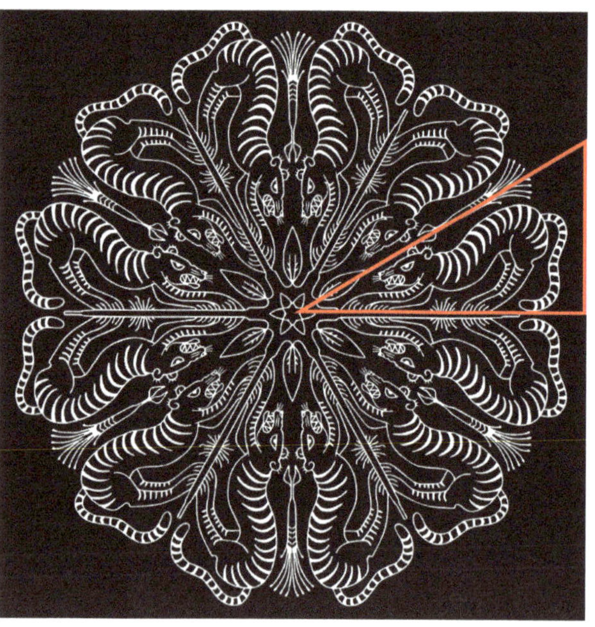

STEP-TWO: Go to the very center of the design, and make lines to make a triangle that goes out to the edge of the drawing. The triangle encompasses one segment.

In the image to the left, you can see that there are 6 segments.

Each one has a very stylized wolf and a plant within it, as well as a part of the light coming from the 6-pointed star above it.

In the next image, there are 6 segments, and each one has 2 images within it. So you cut the segment in half again, to find the fierce tiger.

You might think these are pretty complex.

But imagine having tiles like these - maybe in blue - as a back-splash behind a stove, or as a border on a wall. How fun it could be to contemplate what's in those pictures as you cook or eat breakfast!

Or maybe you have one 8" tile in a nice wood frame, used as a trivet or hot plate.

Or perhaps a set of 4 tiles set into the table - what a wonderful conversation starter as you sit eating at the dinner table. Can you find the musicians?

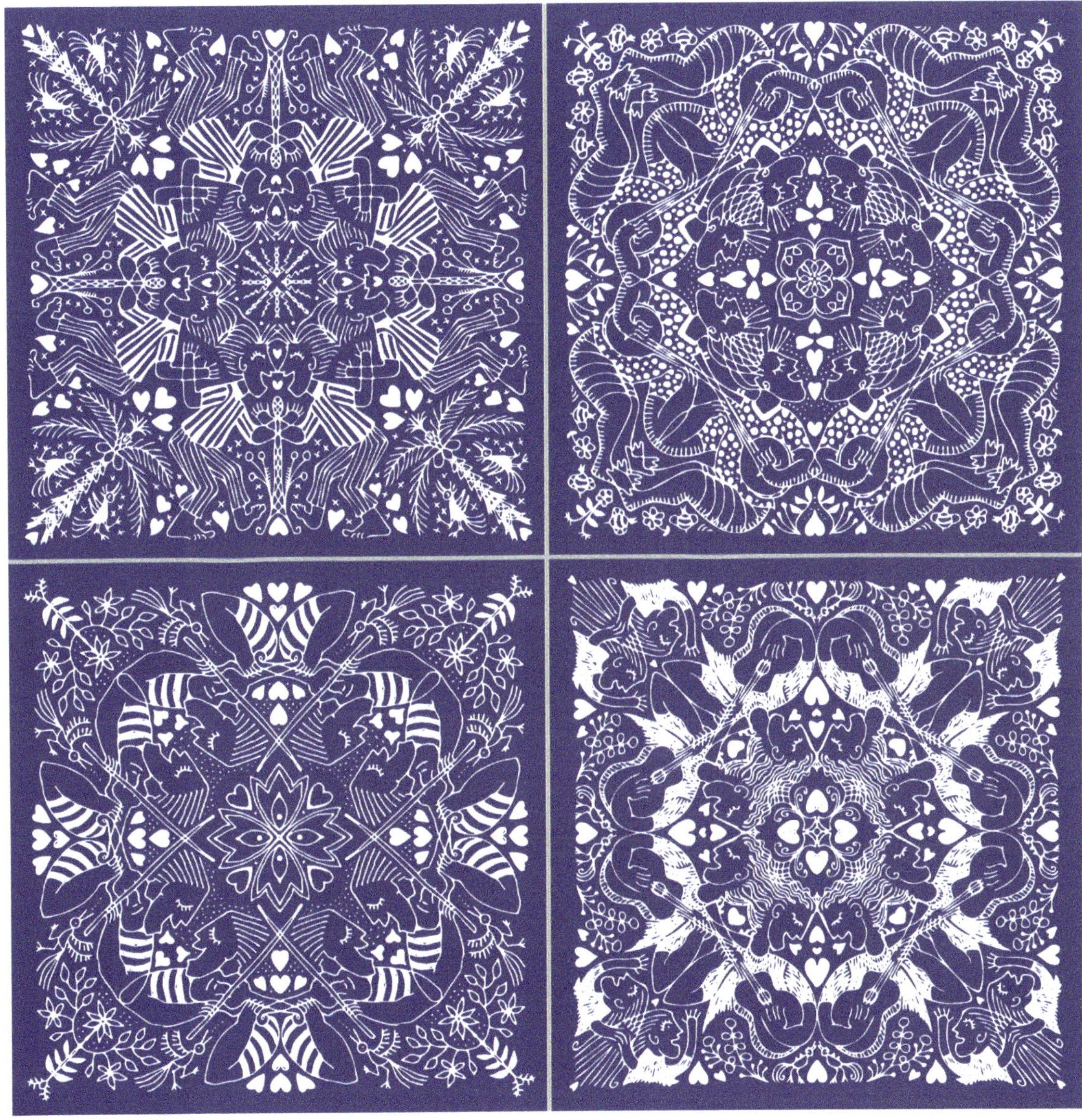

STEP-TWO *(cont.)***:** Go to the center of the design, and make a triangle back out to the edge of the drawing that encompasses just one segment. In each image below, you can see that there are 4 segments.

Each segment has 2 images within it. Cut the segment in half again, to find the main characters, and see what they are doing.

LEFT: the guy sits outside near the garden, bees flying all around, playing his banjo and singing a love song.

RIGHT: that's me, stumbling across the blinding floor to get the coffee pot going in the morning, the birdies making their regular racket outside my window.

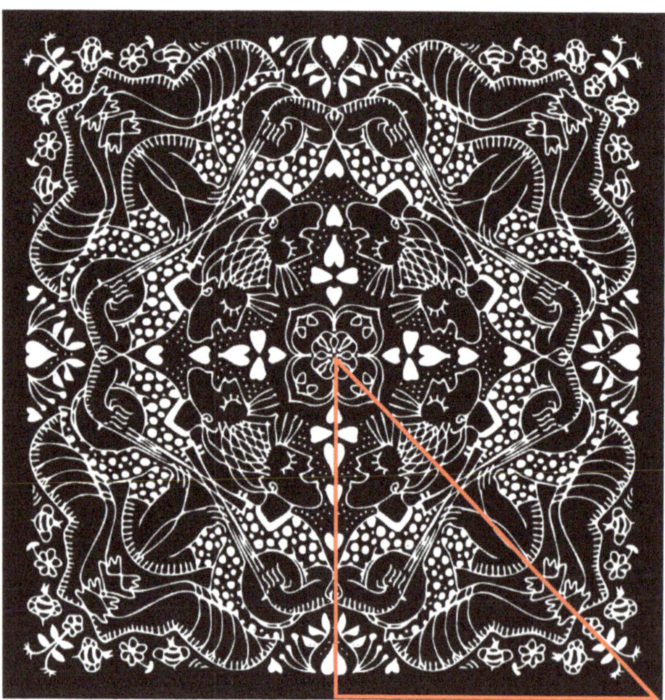

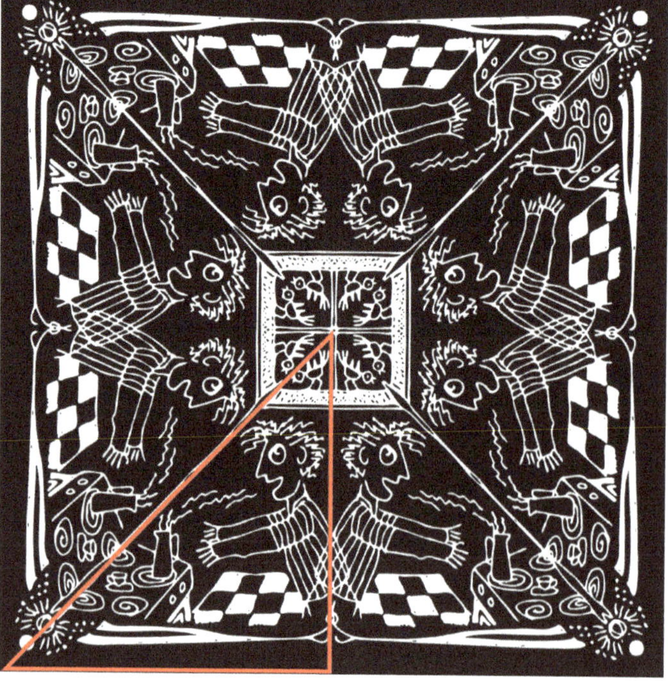

Here are two more images to practice your *seeing* on.

LEFT: I promote ocean clean-up and clean practices on one of my Facebook pages, and do a bunch of sealife drawings as a result. It's now easy to see the dolphins swimming and splashing in the waves, right? If you look closer still, following the red dots, you can see their overlapping fins.

RIGHT: This is from one of my coloring books that was a series on loving one another. In this one, a circle of women are celebrating love for all things.

See how this triangle method works? I hope you enjoy the images in the book more now that you know how to find the characters!

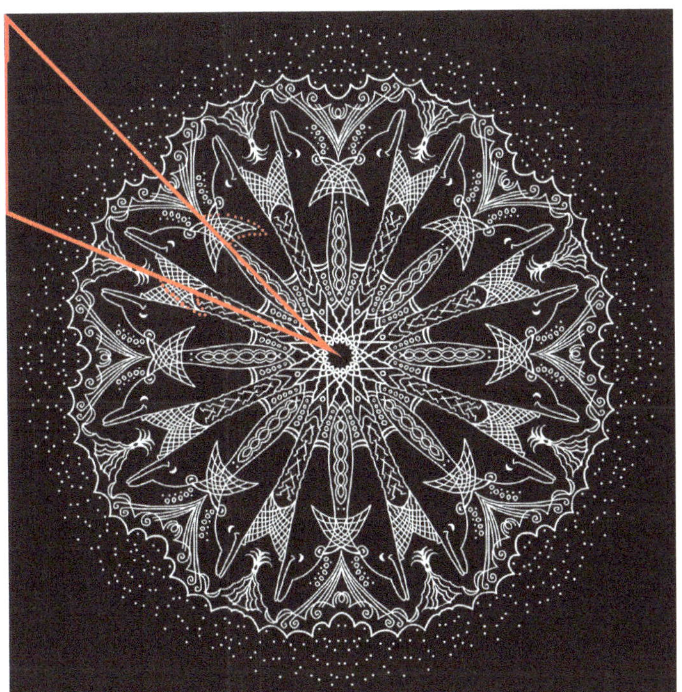

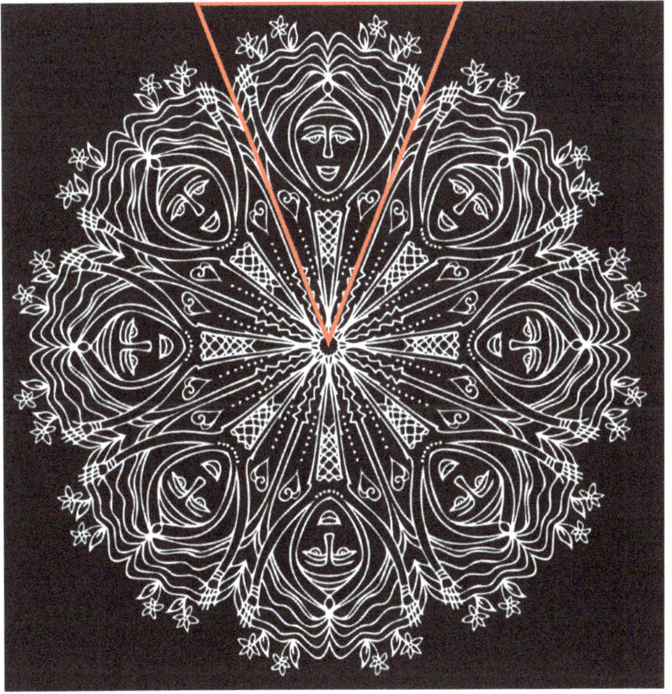

So many uses for these designs!

Straight Illustration: Wall art like posters, framed prints; murals, magazine spot art; book covers, journal covers...

Tiles: all kinds and sizes and colors for splash boards, borders, wall covering, floors, trim, hot plates, trivets...

Bolt Fabric for everyday use and fashion...

Clothing & Accessories: Scarves, socks, skirts, dresses, T-shirts, hoodies ... too many others to list. Plus totes, backpacks, duffle bags, handbags, clutches, luggage; phone and computer skins ...

Home Decor: Wall art, wall paper, stickers, shower curtains, bath mats, rugs, tea towels, hand towels, pillows for bed, couch and floor, welcome mats, blankets, duvet covers, bedding, tapestries...

Party Goods: Wrapping paper, ribbon, tissue paper, gift paper, gift cards, gift notes and tags, paper plates, place mats, table runners, table cloths, cups, mugs, napkins...

Stationery: Greeting cards, postcards, business cards, stationery borders, note pads, envelopes, stickers...

Pattern design for fabric

Here is a combination of several designs I created for fabric. This celebrates the Bluegrass band I used to sing in a million years ago!

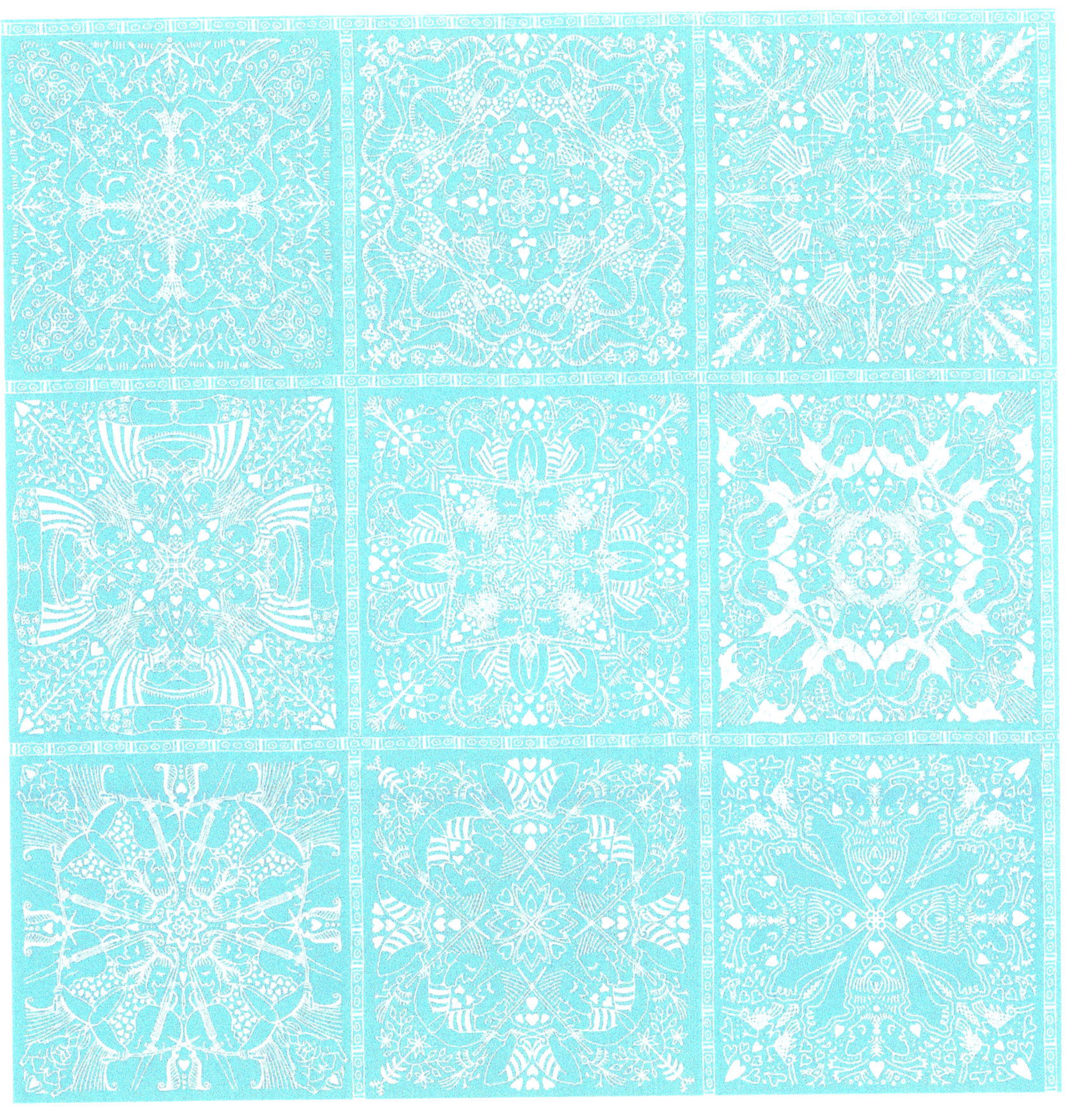

The evolution

When I first began doing pattern design for this year, I was making images with a lot of flowers and kind of abstracted shapes. Like these:

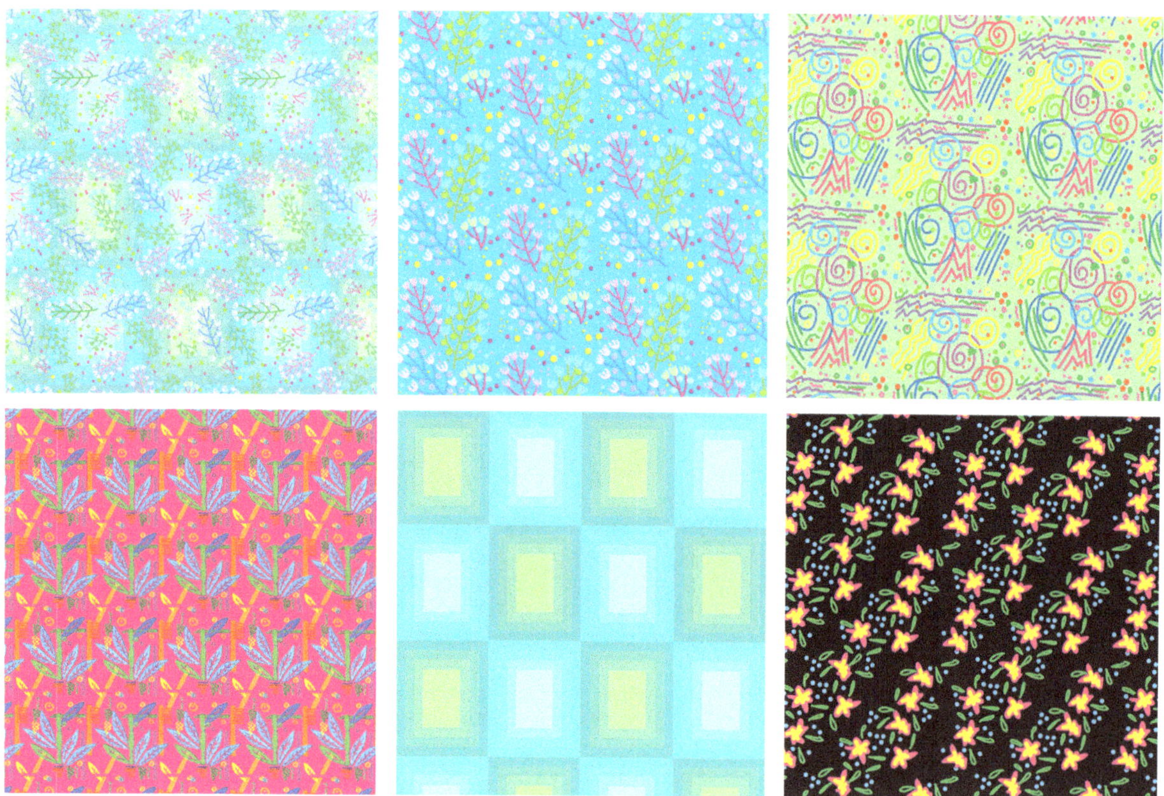

Something was missing though. I wanted them to be fun - and they were close, but not FUN. So just to relax one afternoon, I started doodling, and the first Story drawing emerged. Now *that* was fun! I did more, and more, until now at this writing there are over 100!

I have been surprised...

Over the time it took for me to create these latest images, I've noticed myself wandering into some specific categories of drawings.

Rather than cute images for young kids clothes or toys, or seasonal or holiday themes, I lean towards these:

Geometric: Ideas, feelings, concepts
Nature: Sky, Plants, Animals, Fish, Birds
Humans Doing: Love, Music, Food, Sports

They tend to be either abstractly stylized (like the dolphins and the little owl drawing at the very beginning of the book), or images from day-to-day life that I find comforting or funny.

I hope you get as much enjoyment out of these drawings as I have!

Much aloha -

Angela

Angela Treat Lyon
Chico, California 2021

A little treat

I wanted to add this photograph of Monet's kitchen in his house in Giverny, France. I really had to laugh when I saw it - my first thought was, "have a few tiles, Monet?" Just goes to show you can never get enough tiles....

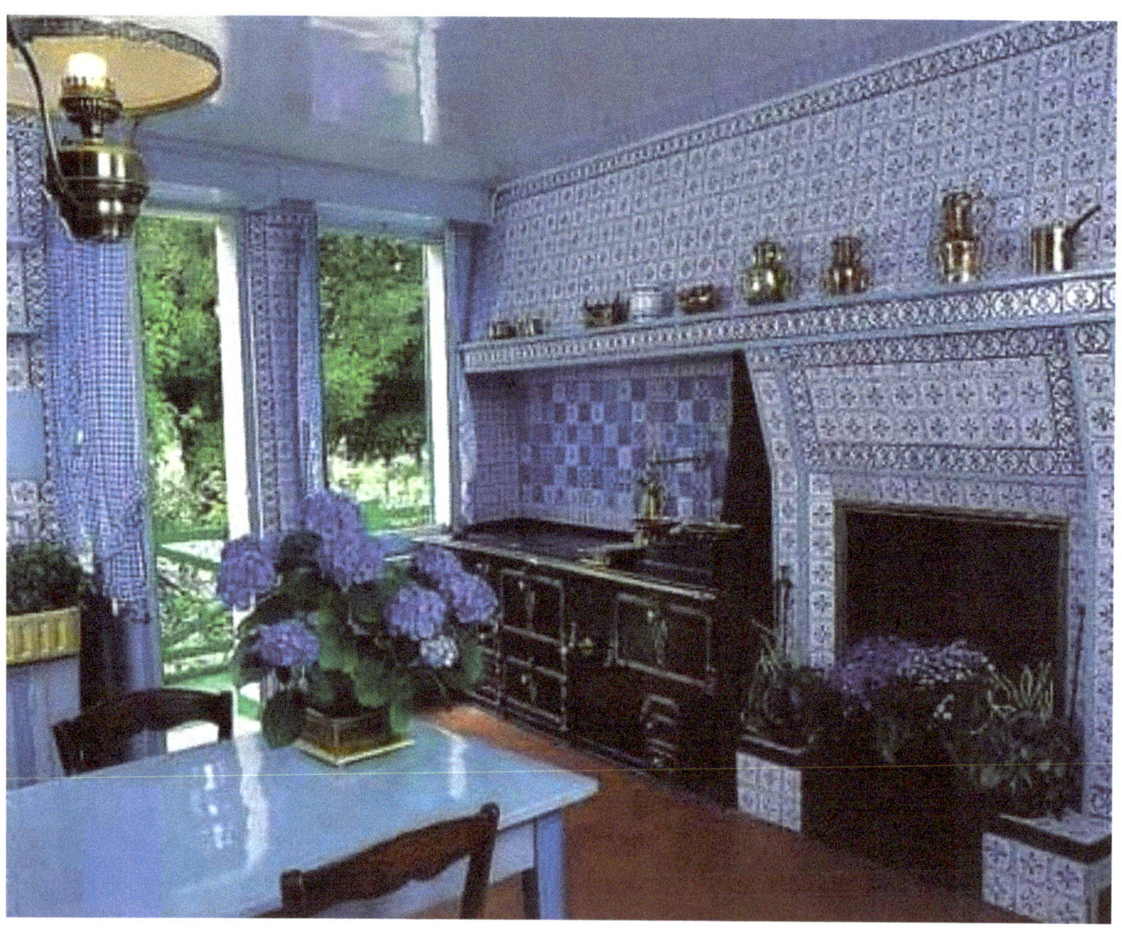

Contents

Contents

Contents

Contents

Story One

The ARTIST

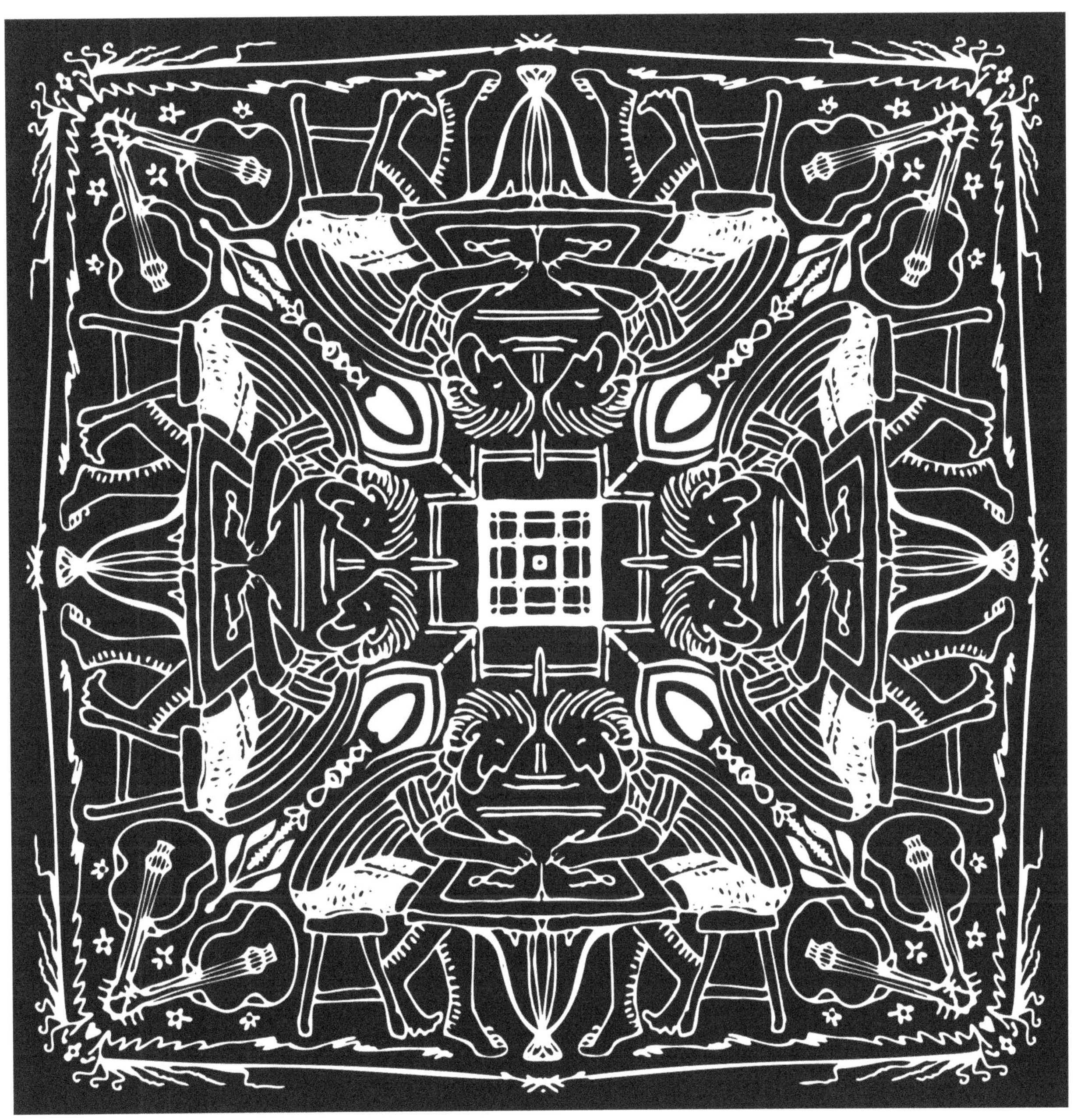

Drawing from the Heart

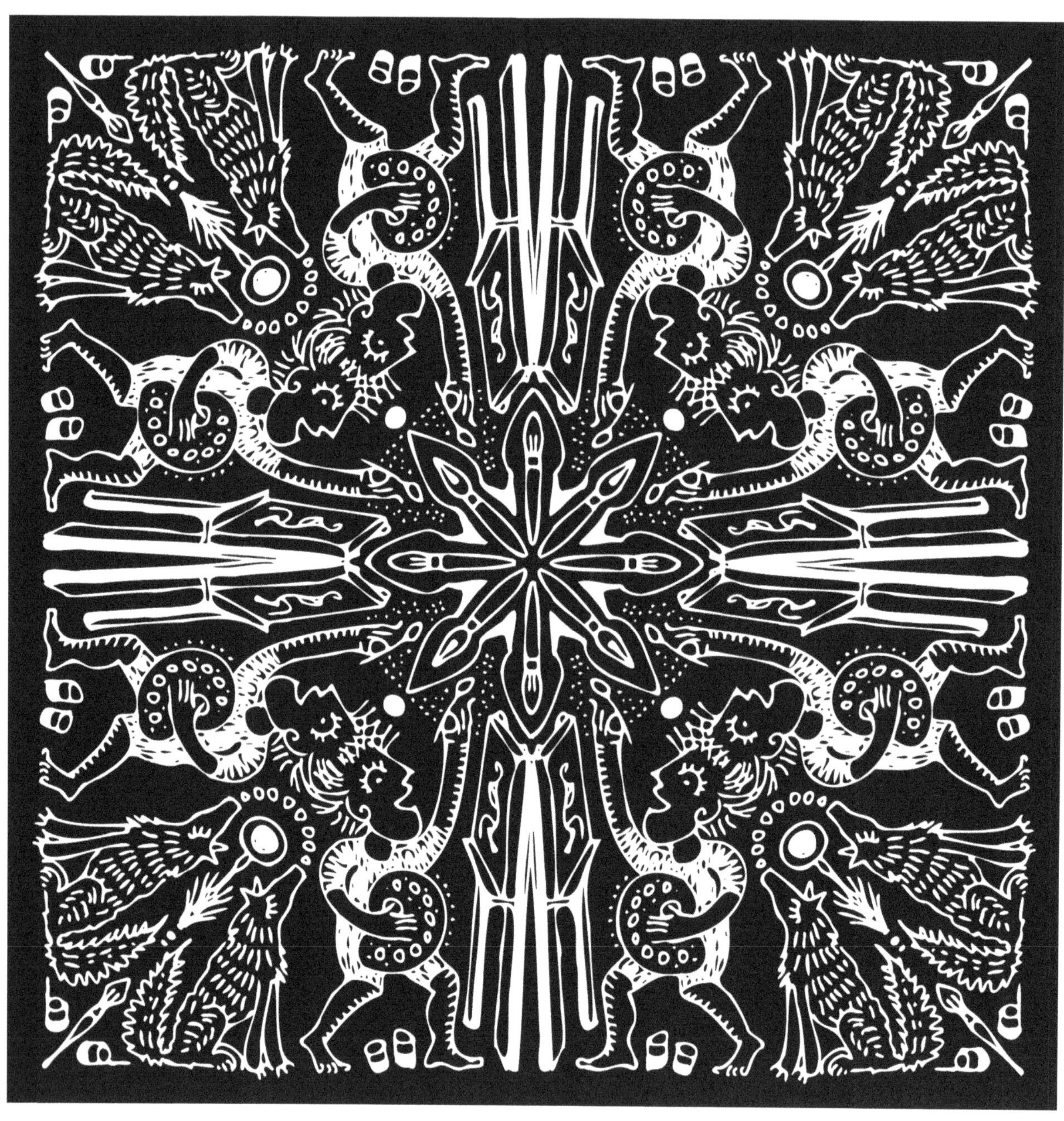

Splashing Paint, Fido Howling

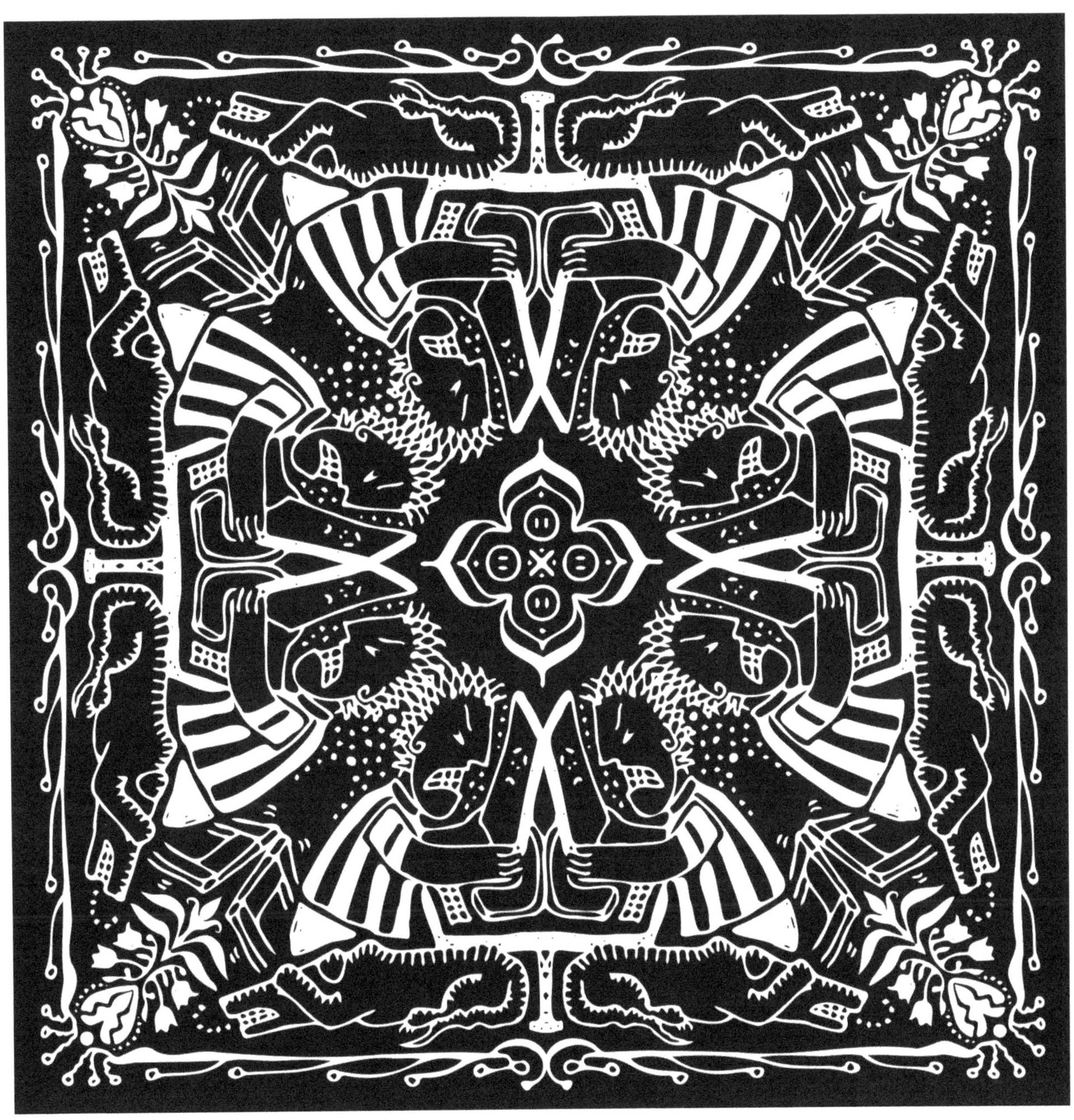

The Technical Struggle

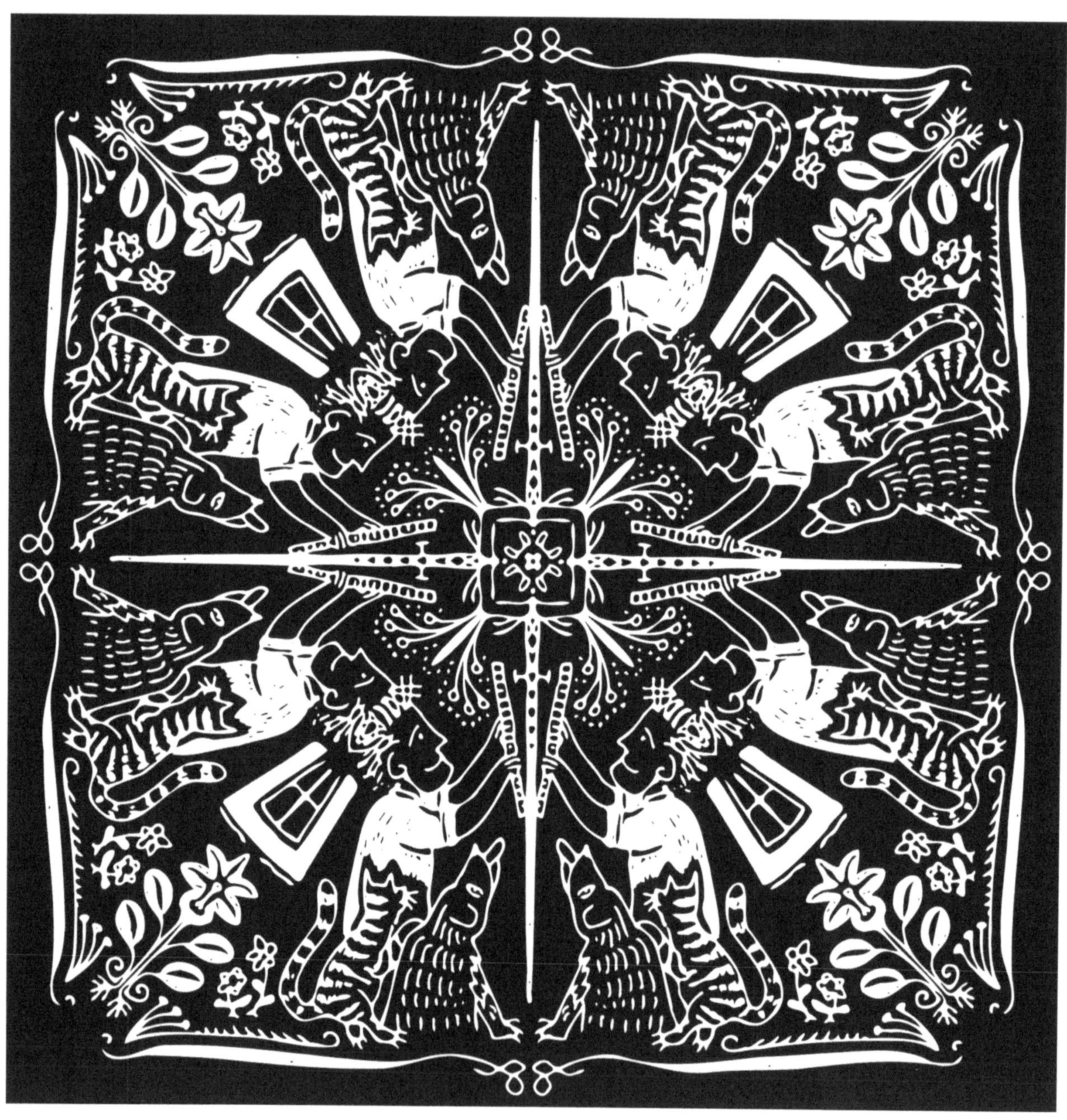

Finally Hanging the Show. Felix and Fido Approve.

Story Two

FIDO

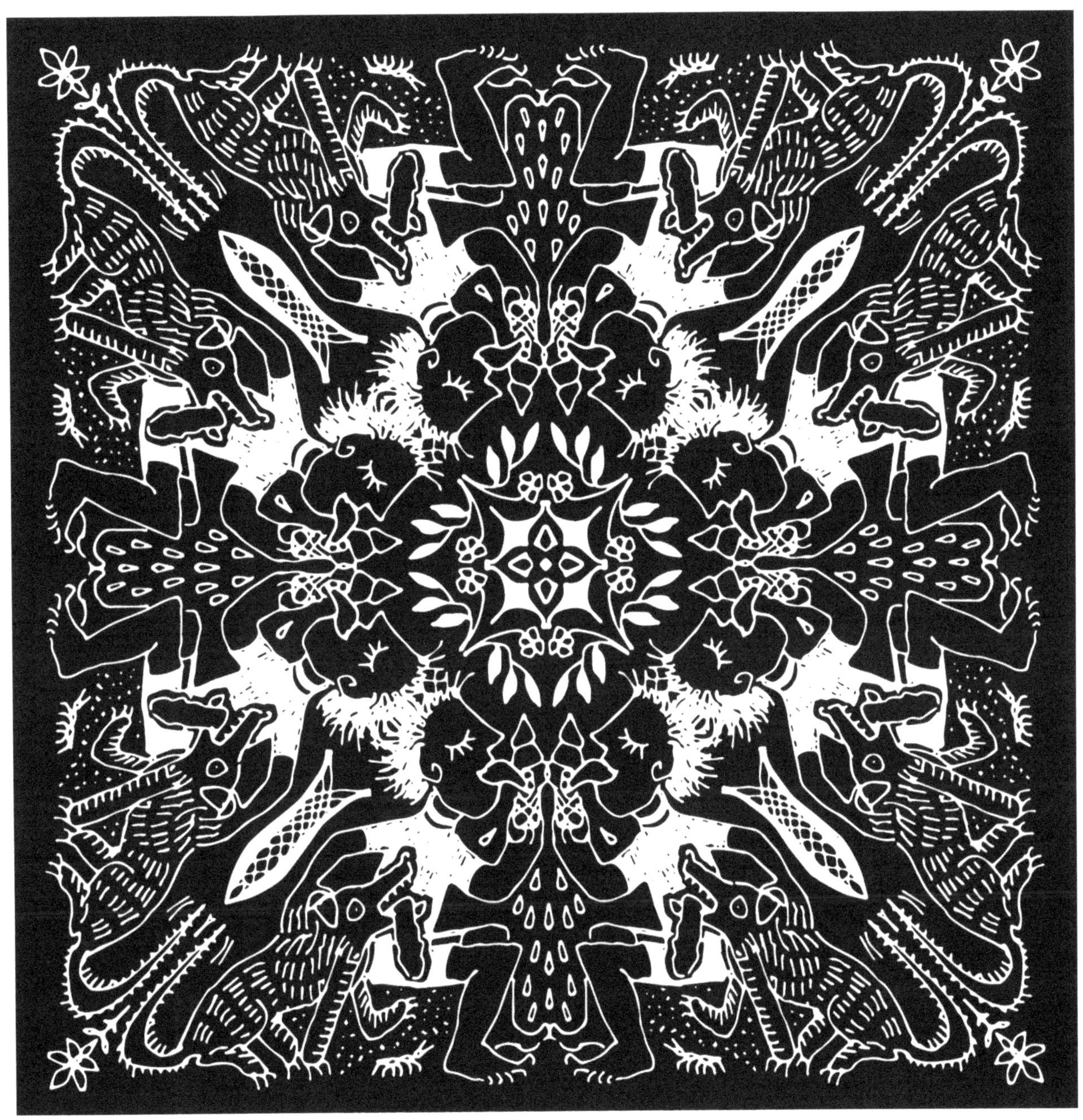

Fido Wants Some Ice Cream, too

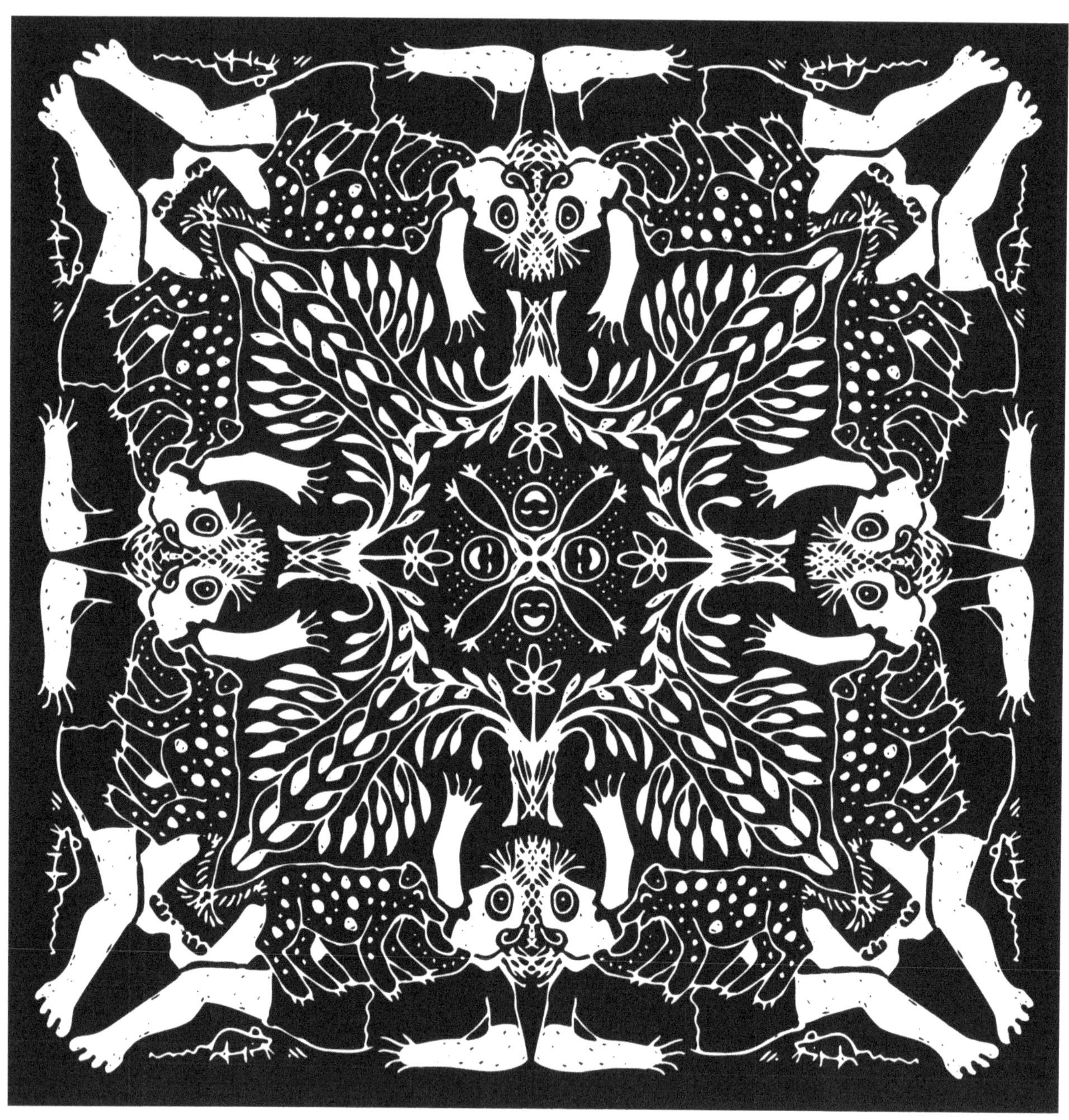

Fido Can't Wait!

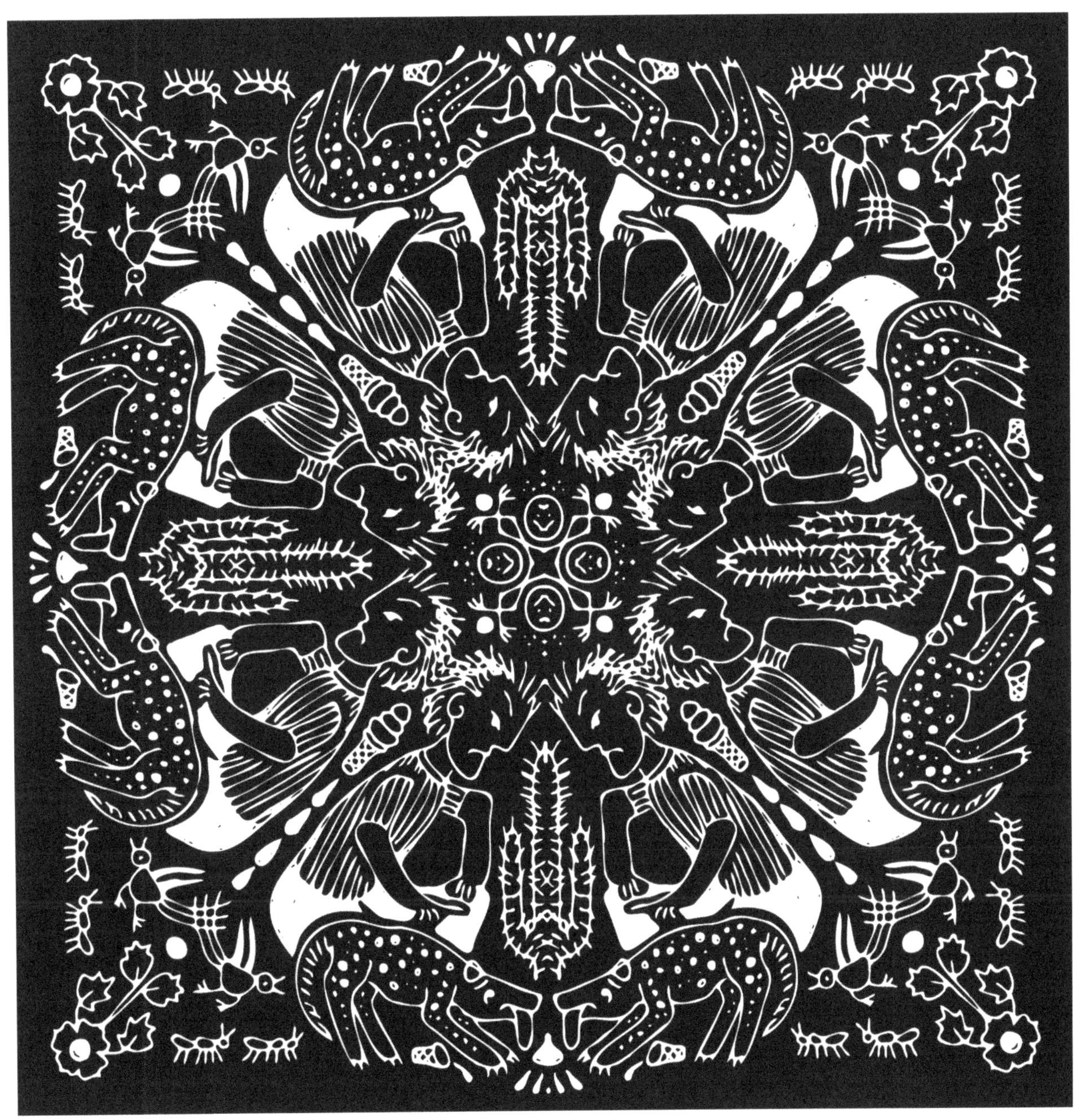

Fido Gets Sick, and then Gets Scolded. Poor Fido.

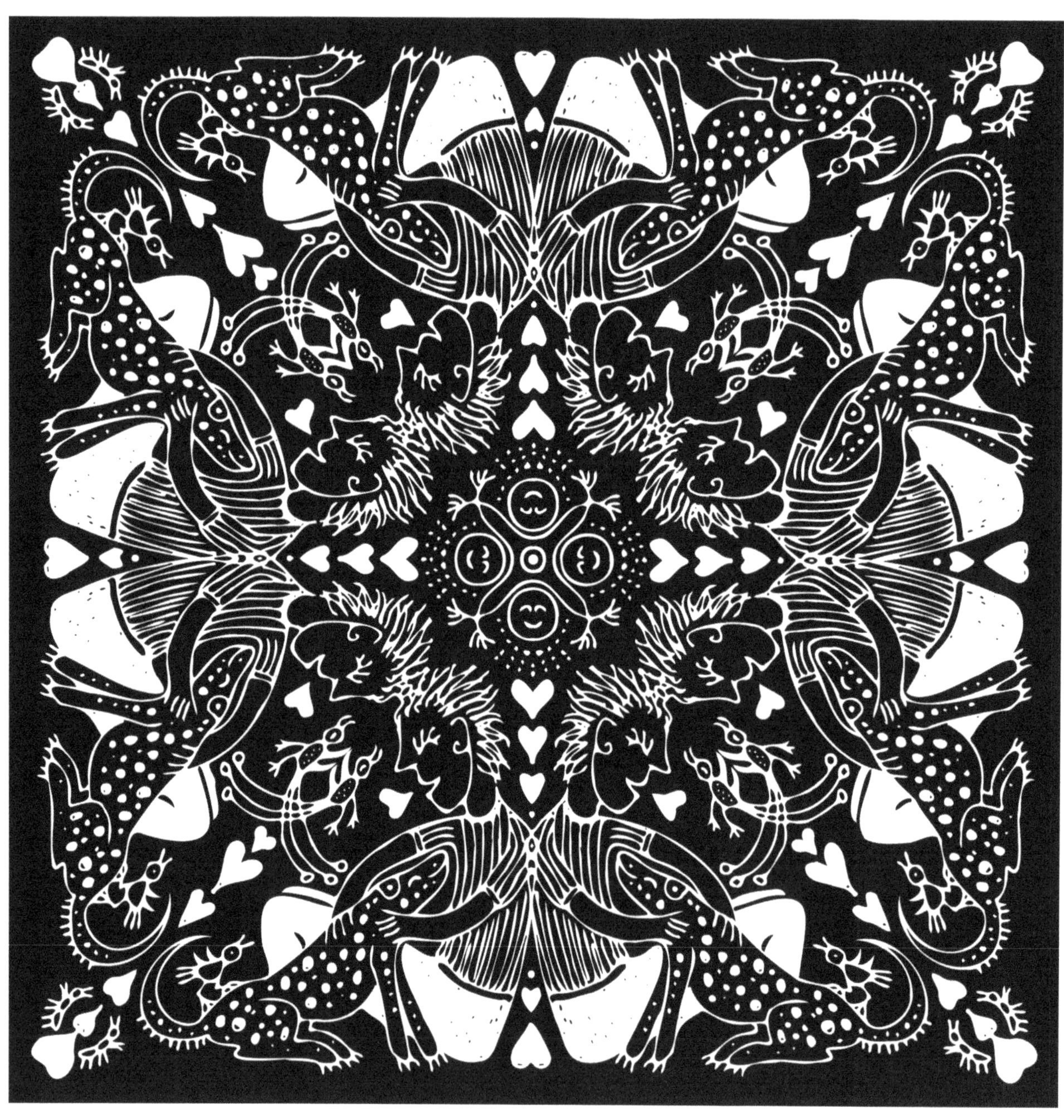

That's OK, Boy! Come Here, I Love You!

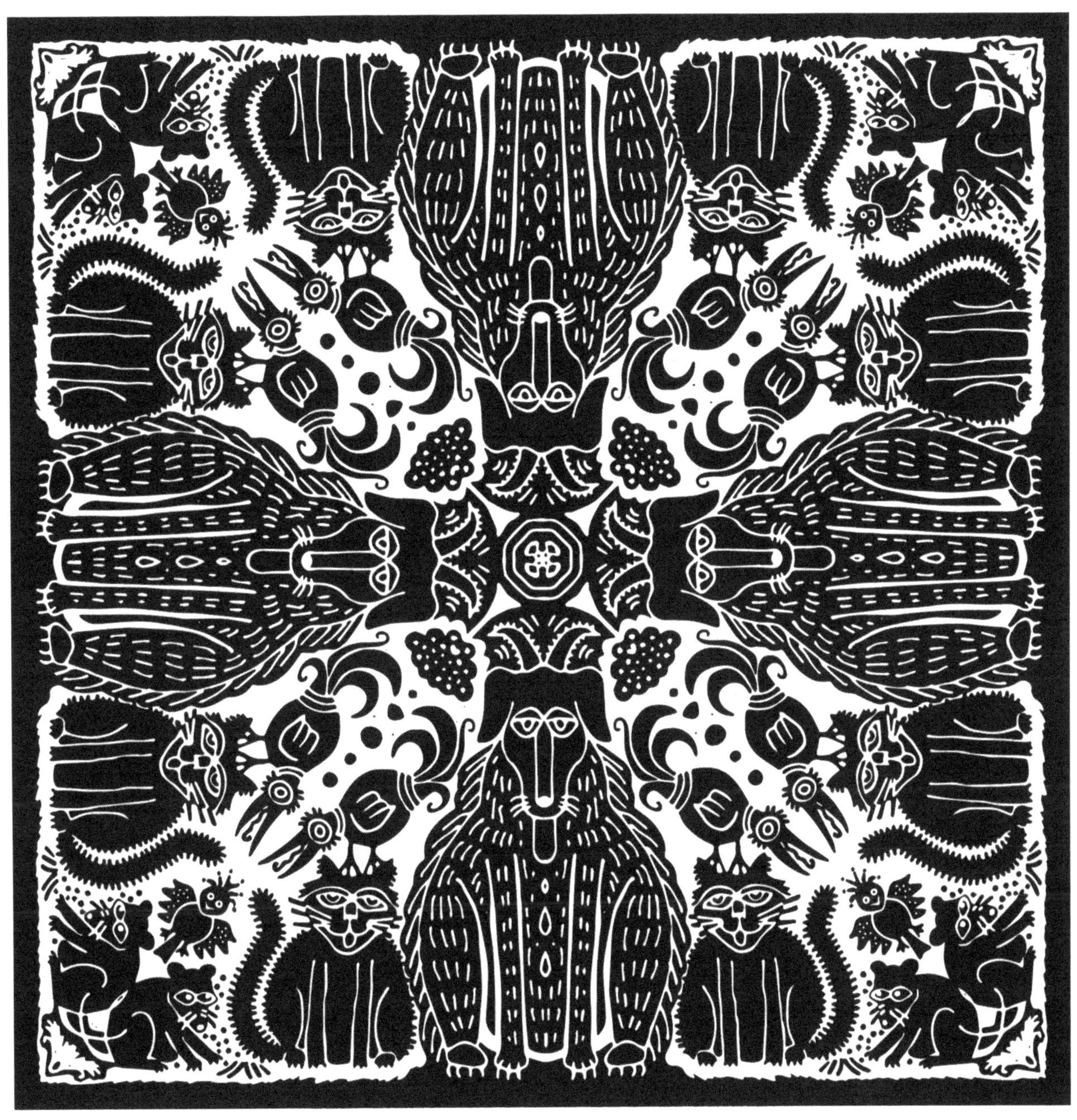

See, Fido? This Could Be Your Future!

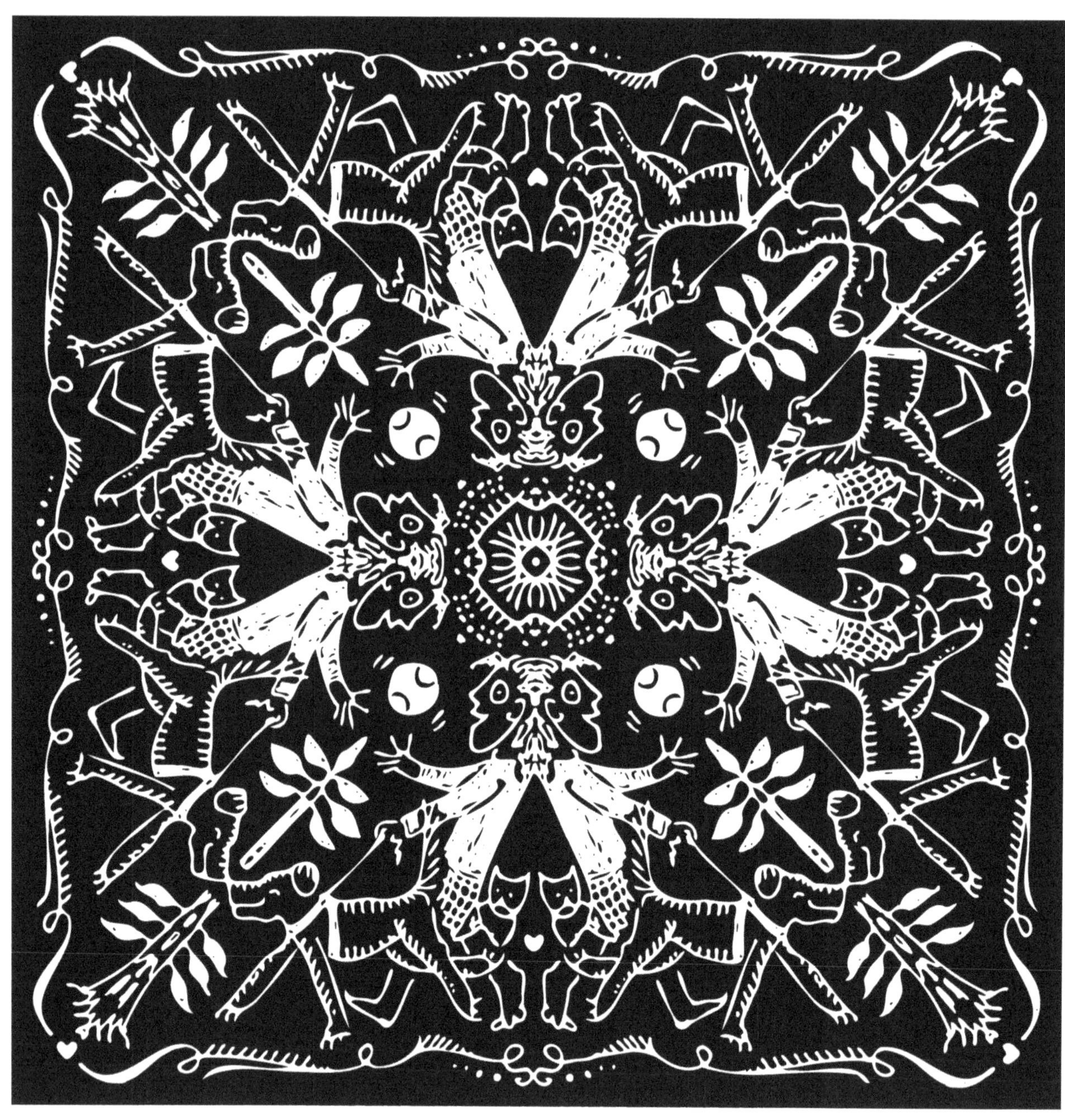

Let's Go Walk All that Ice Cream Off!

Story Three

DINNERTIME

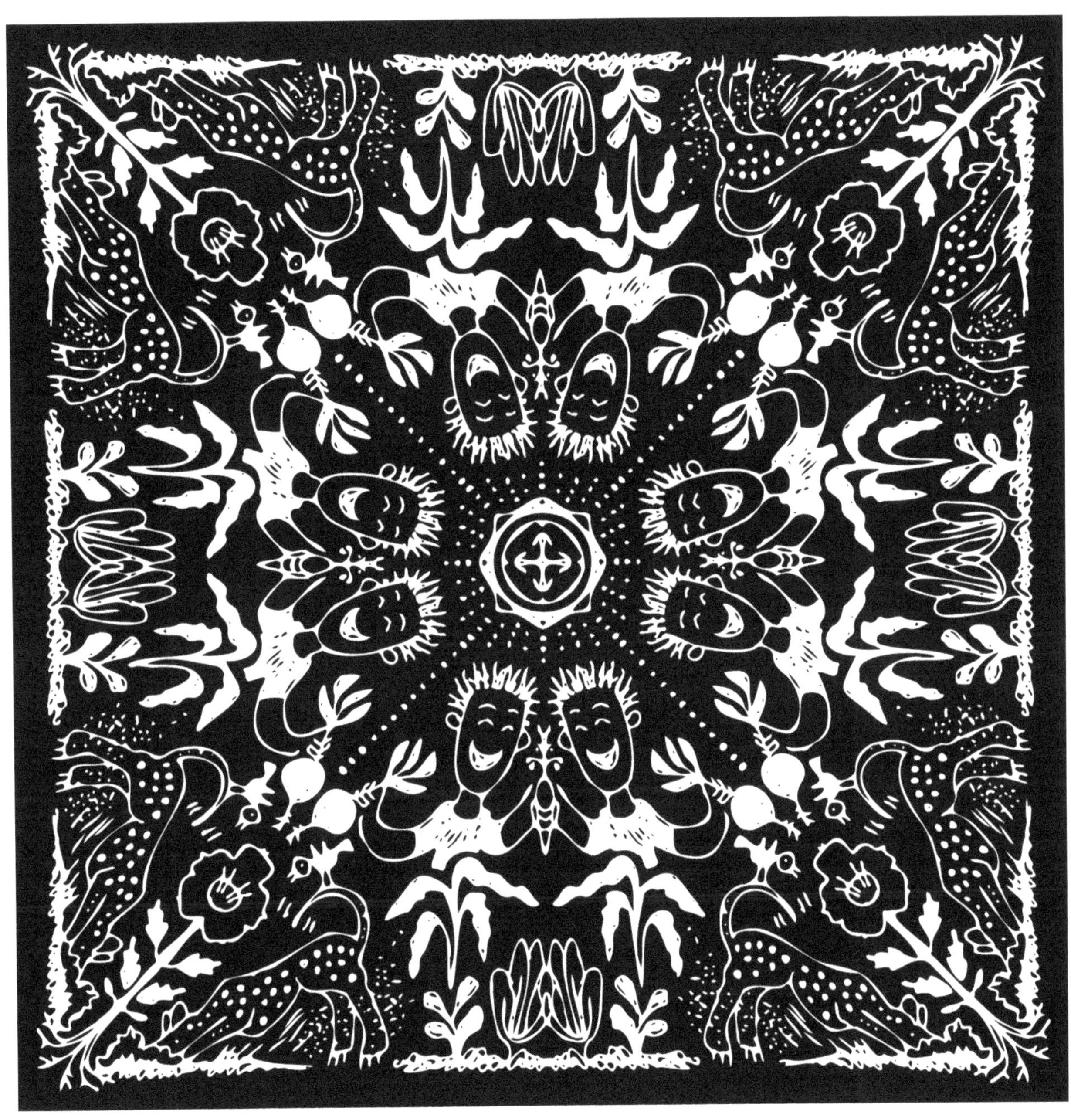

Fido, Got Some Carrots There? Here Are Some Beets...

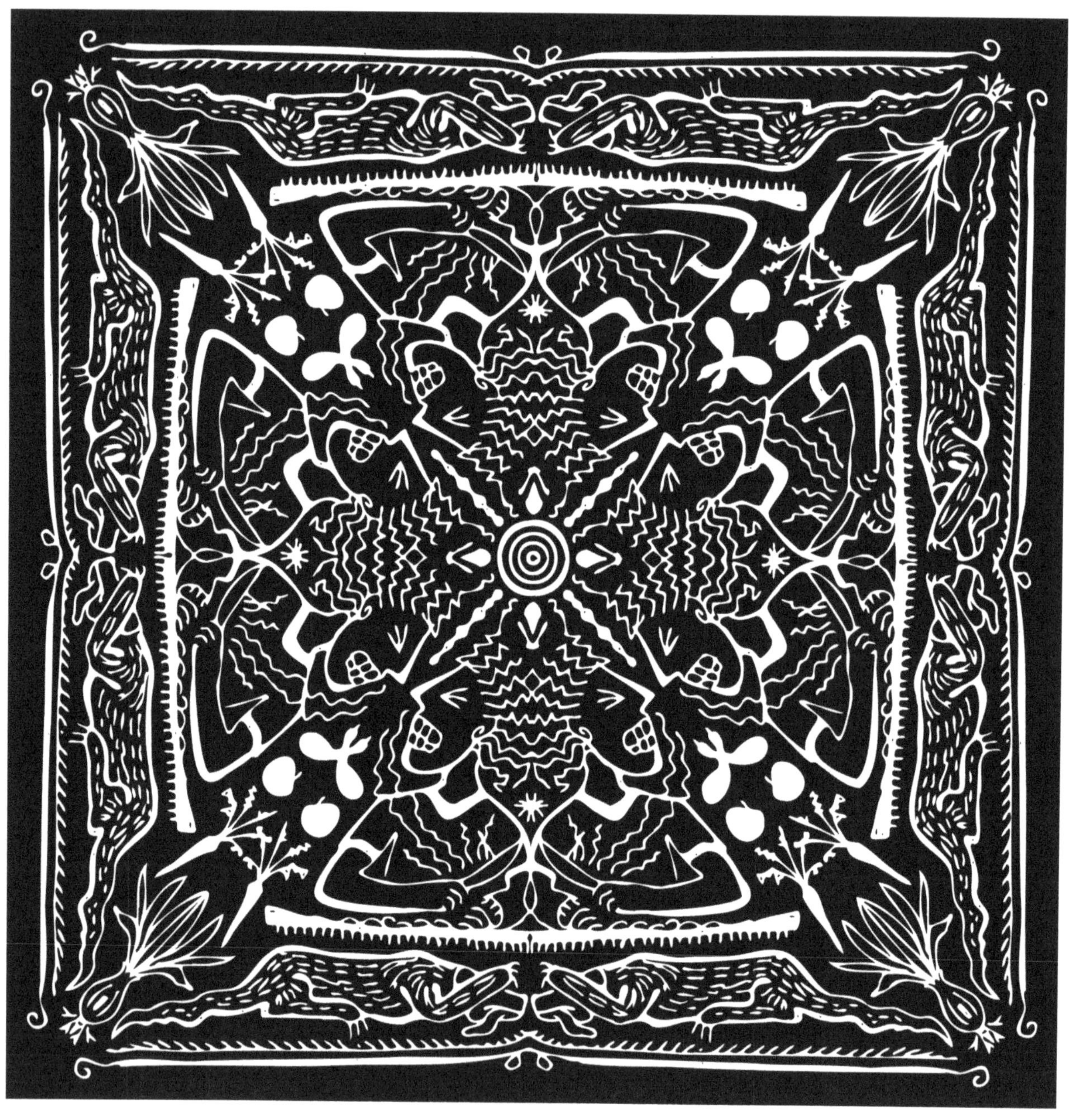

Onions Make Me Cry ... and Fido, too

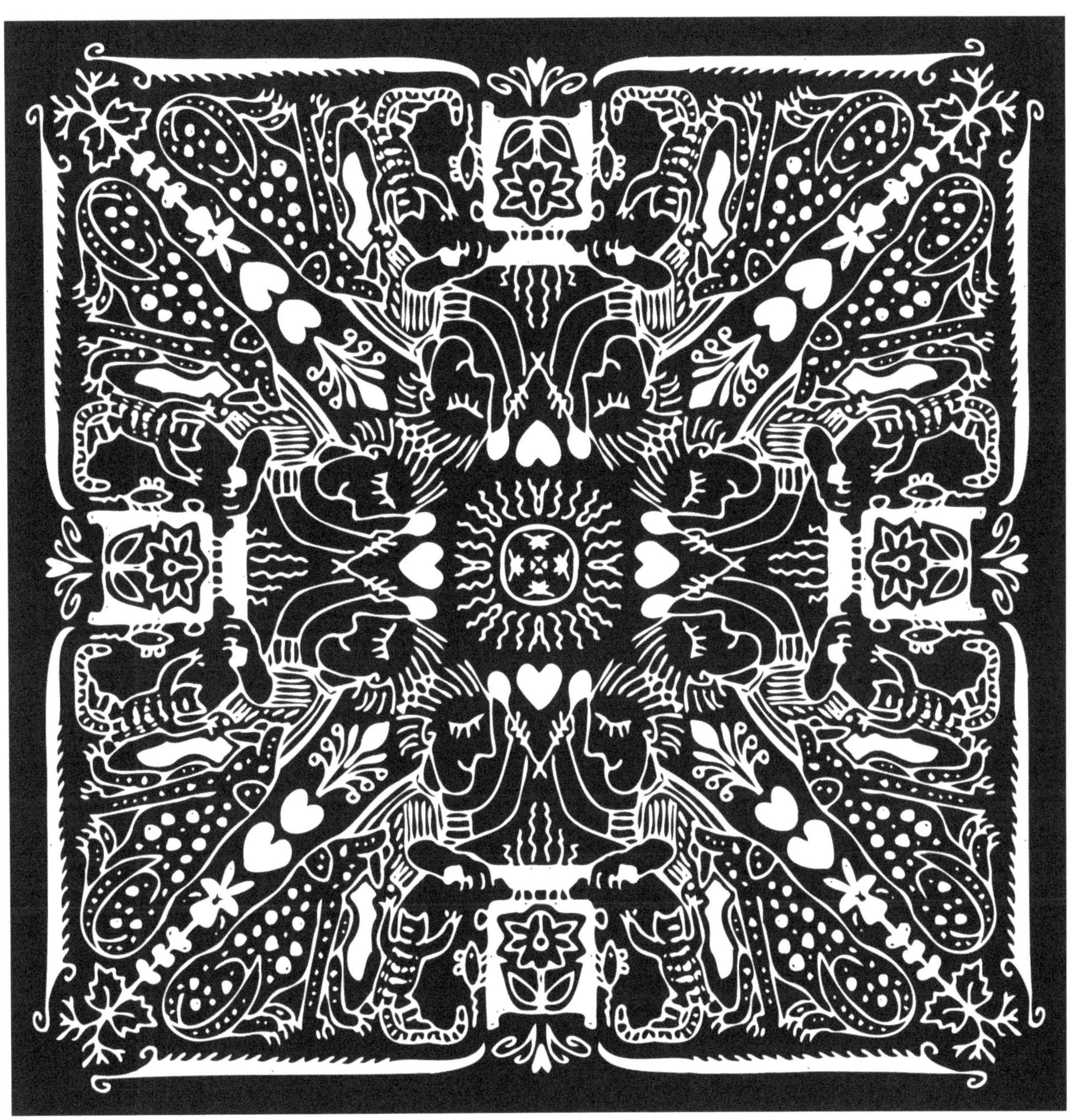

Everyone Wants to Do the Cooking

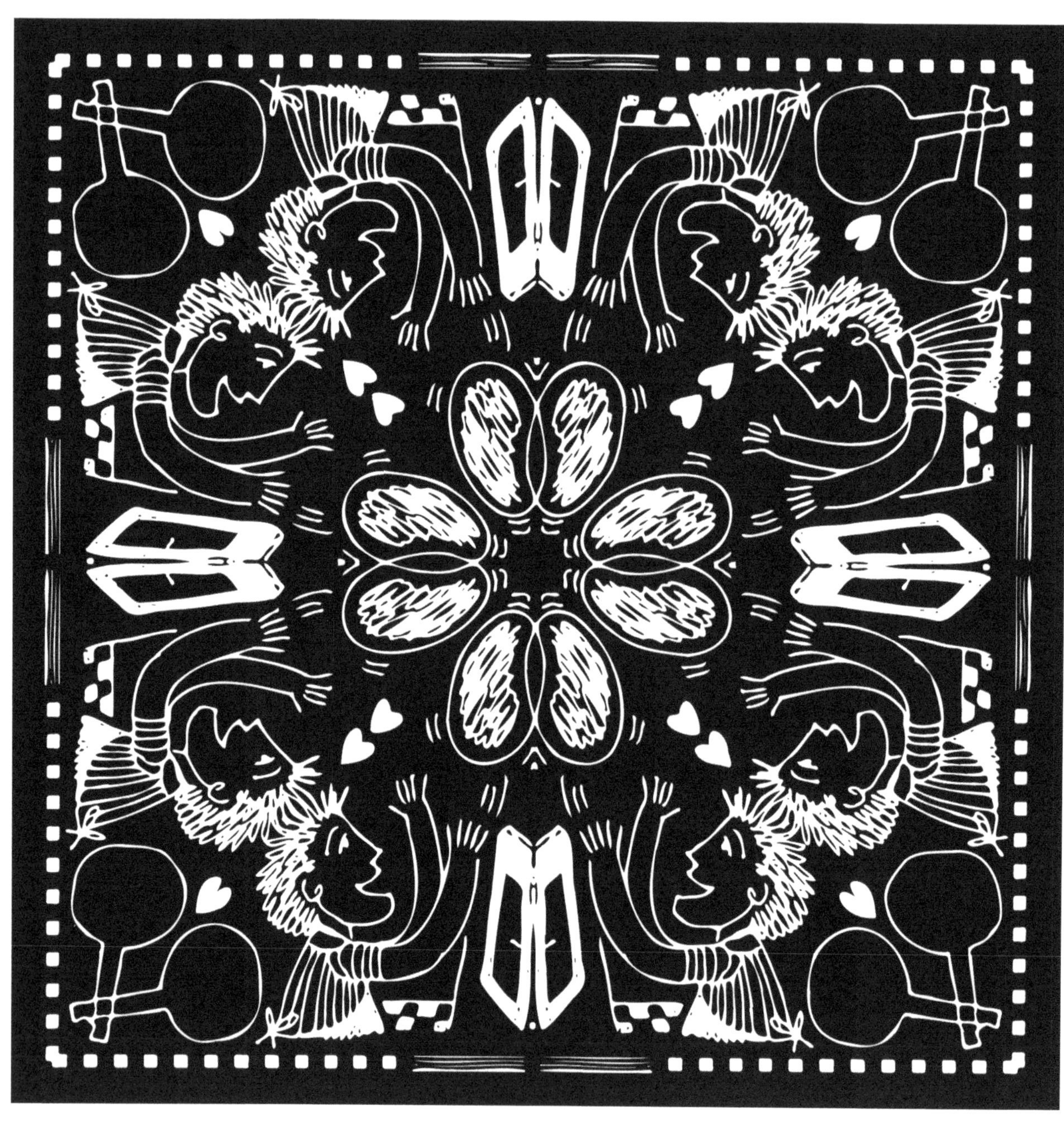

Let's Make Some Pizza!

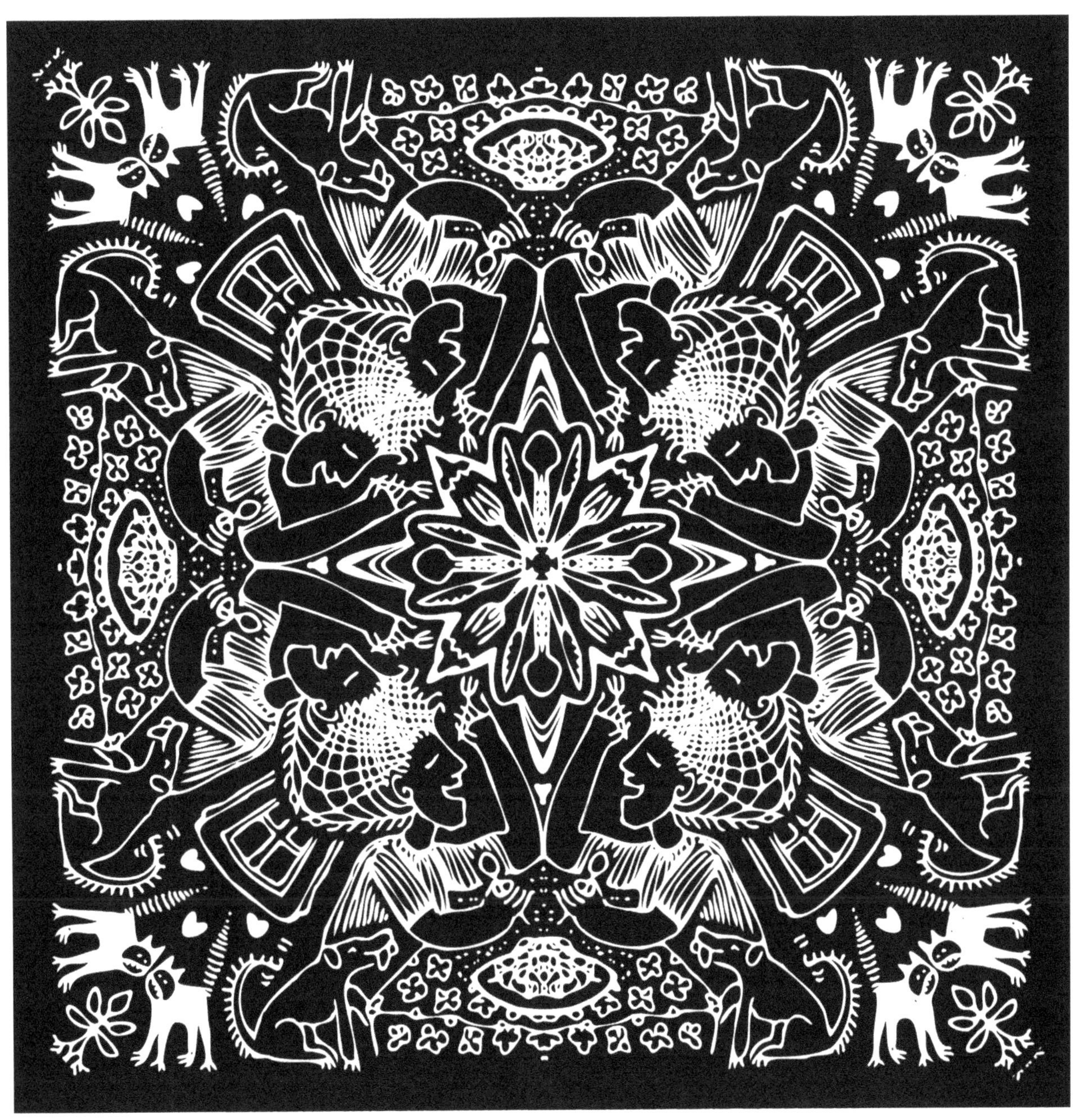

Mmmm, this Spaghetti Is So Good. Felix Disagrees

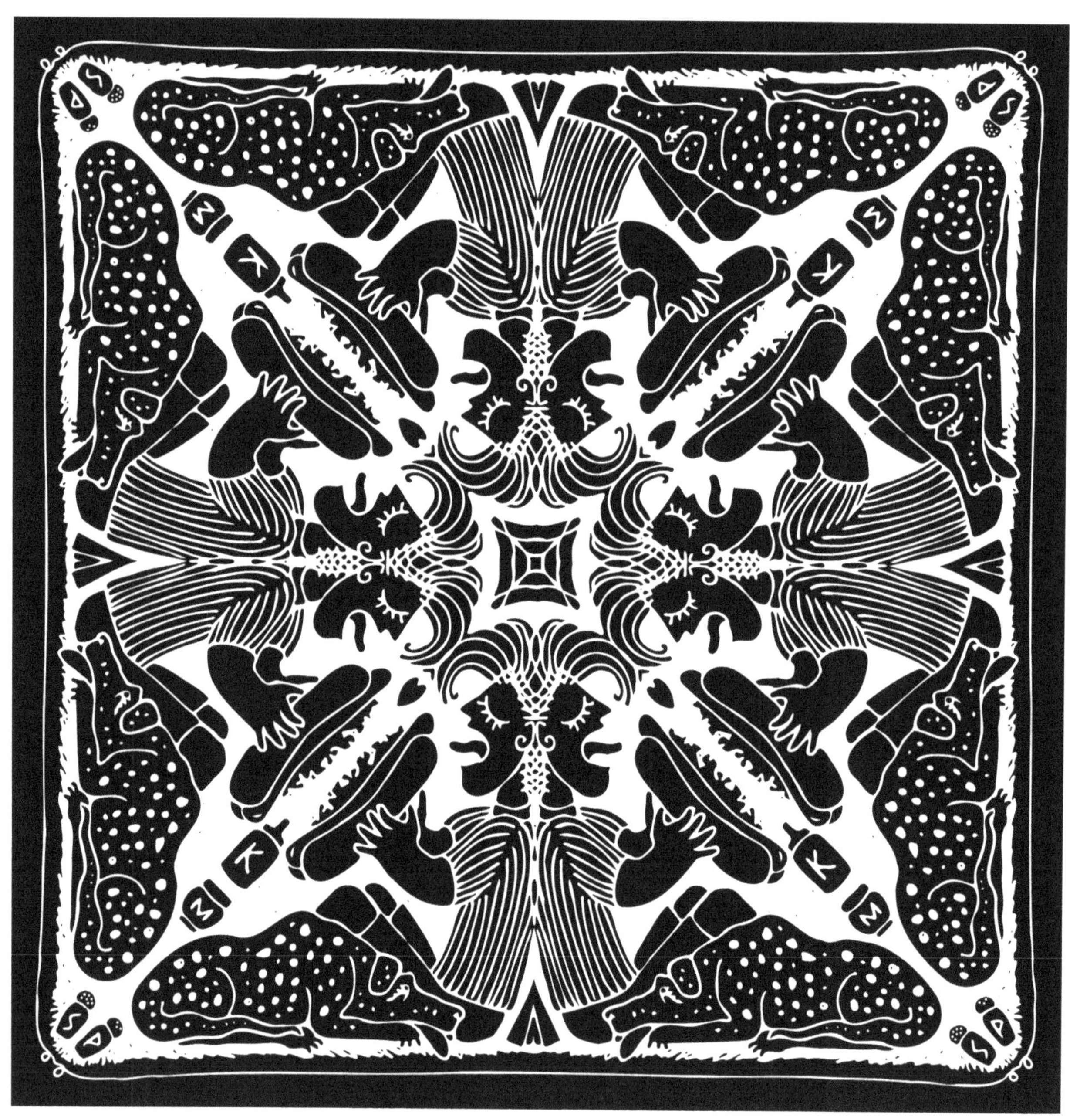

Hot Diggety-Dog - Hot Dogs!

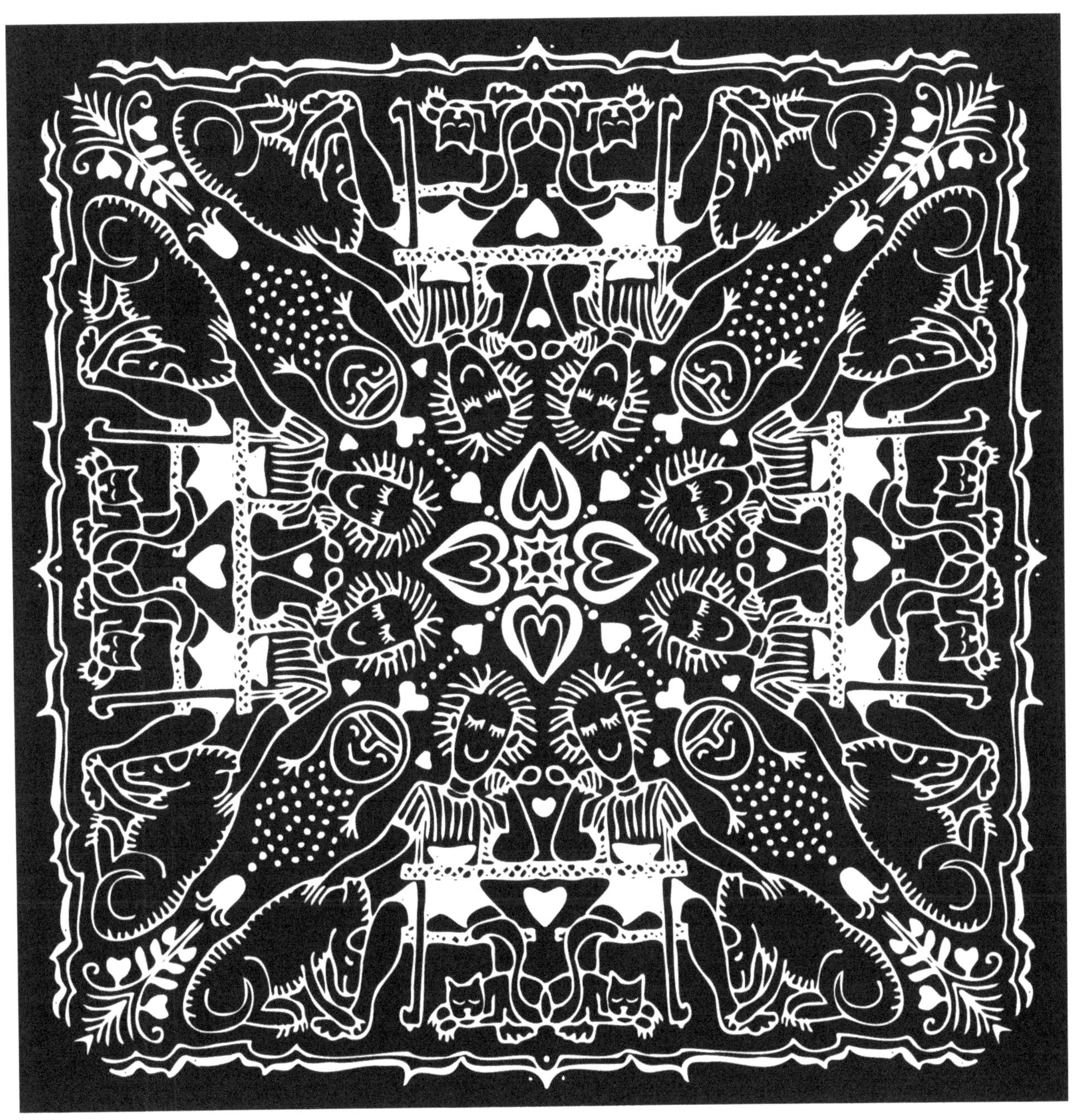

We Are So Full!

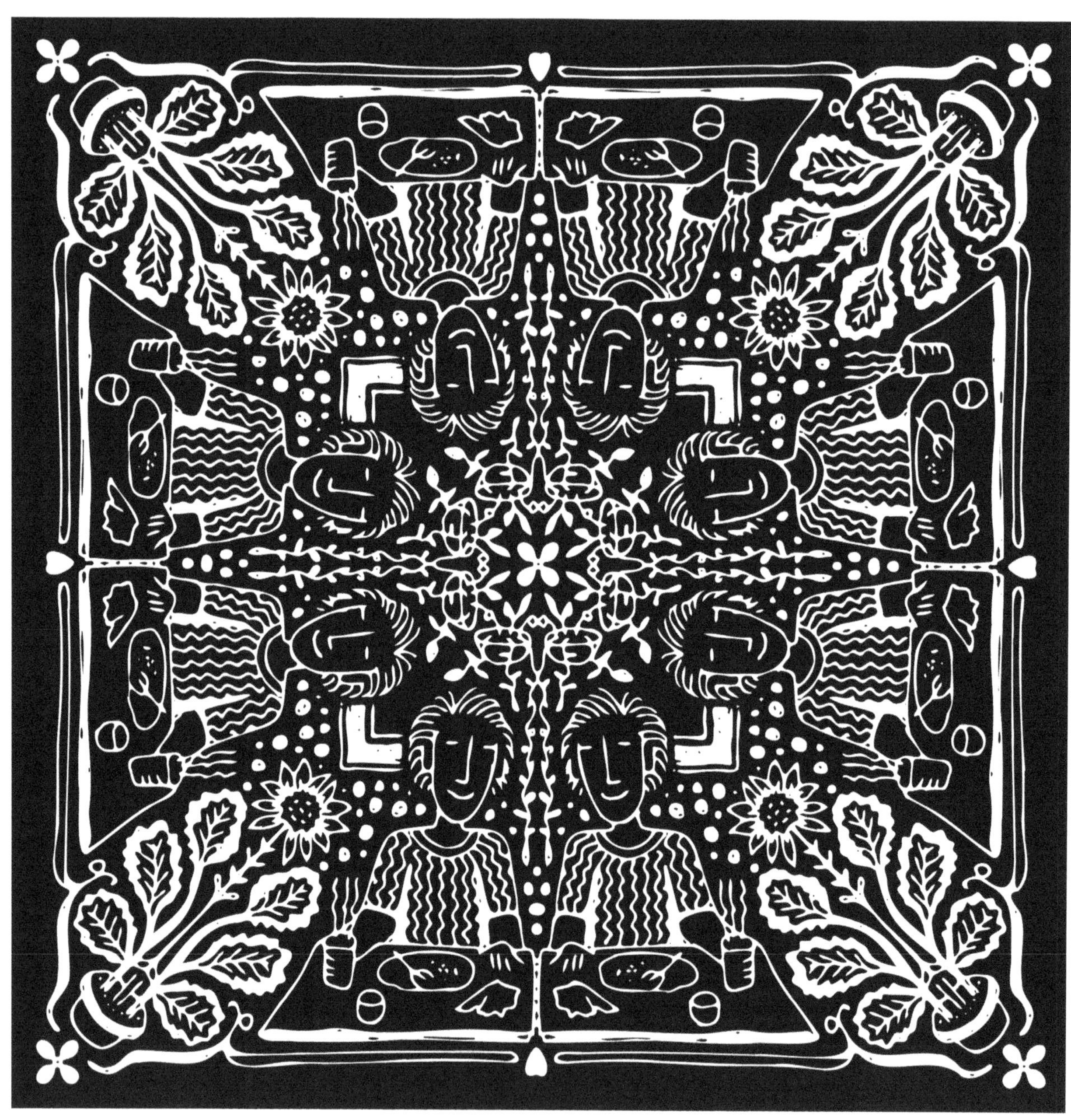

I'm Just Going to Sit A Bit and Savor the Moment...

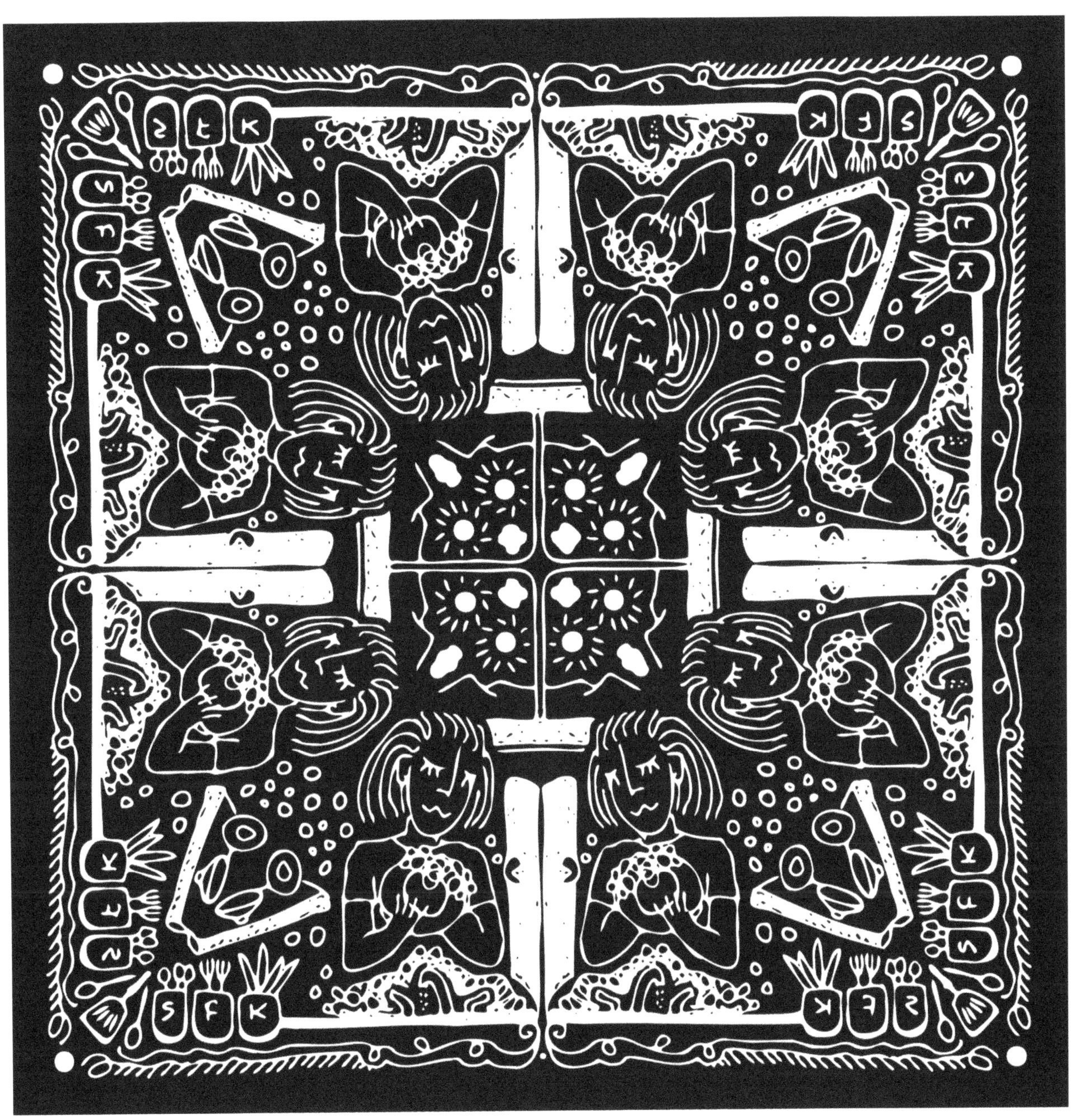

...and then I'm Just Going to Do the Dishes.

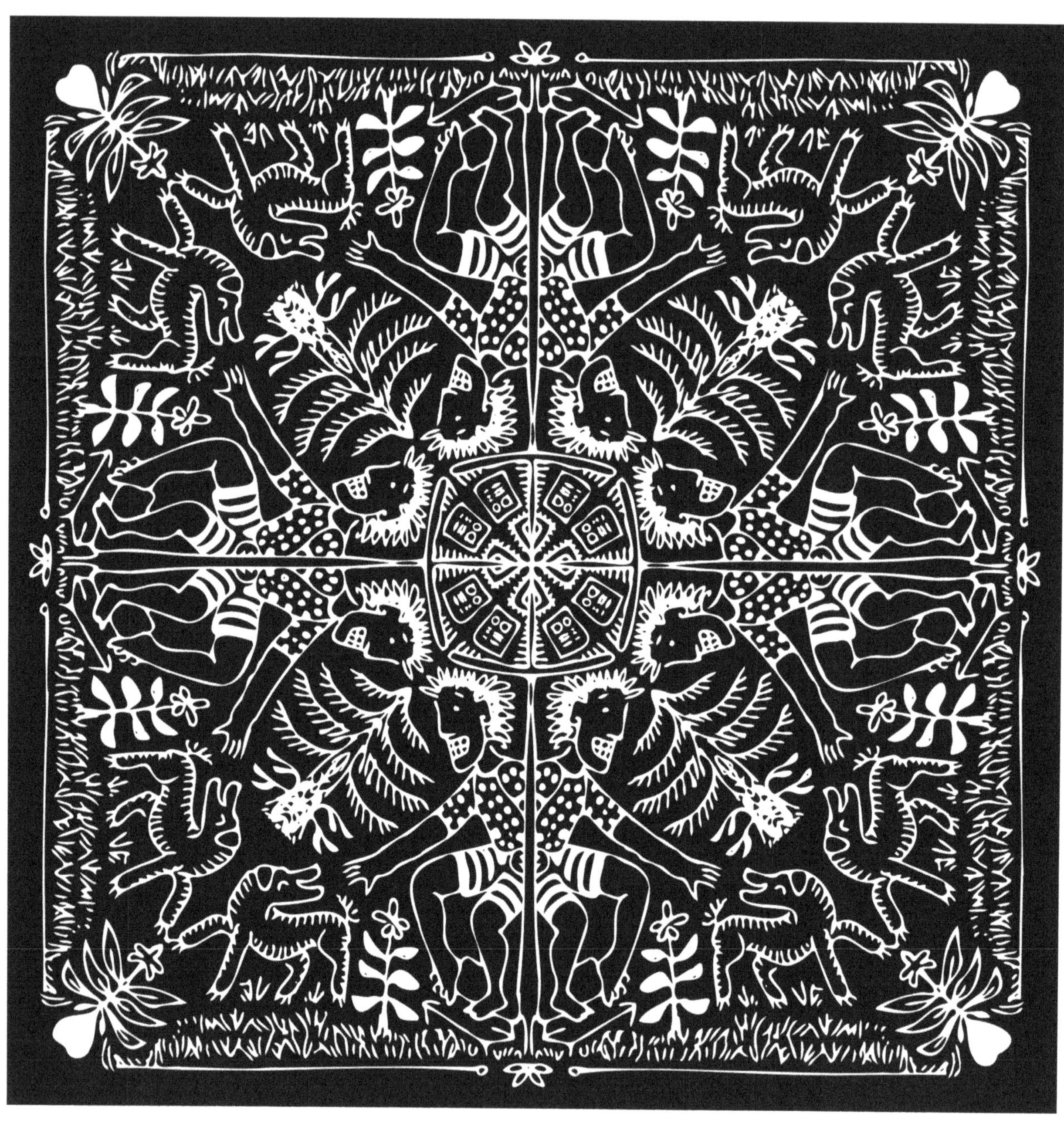

Maybe I'll Ignore My To-Do List and Slip Outside for a Little Walk with Fido...

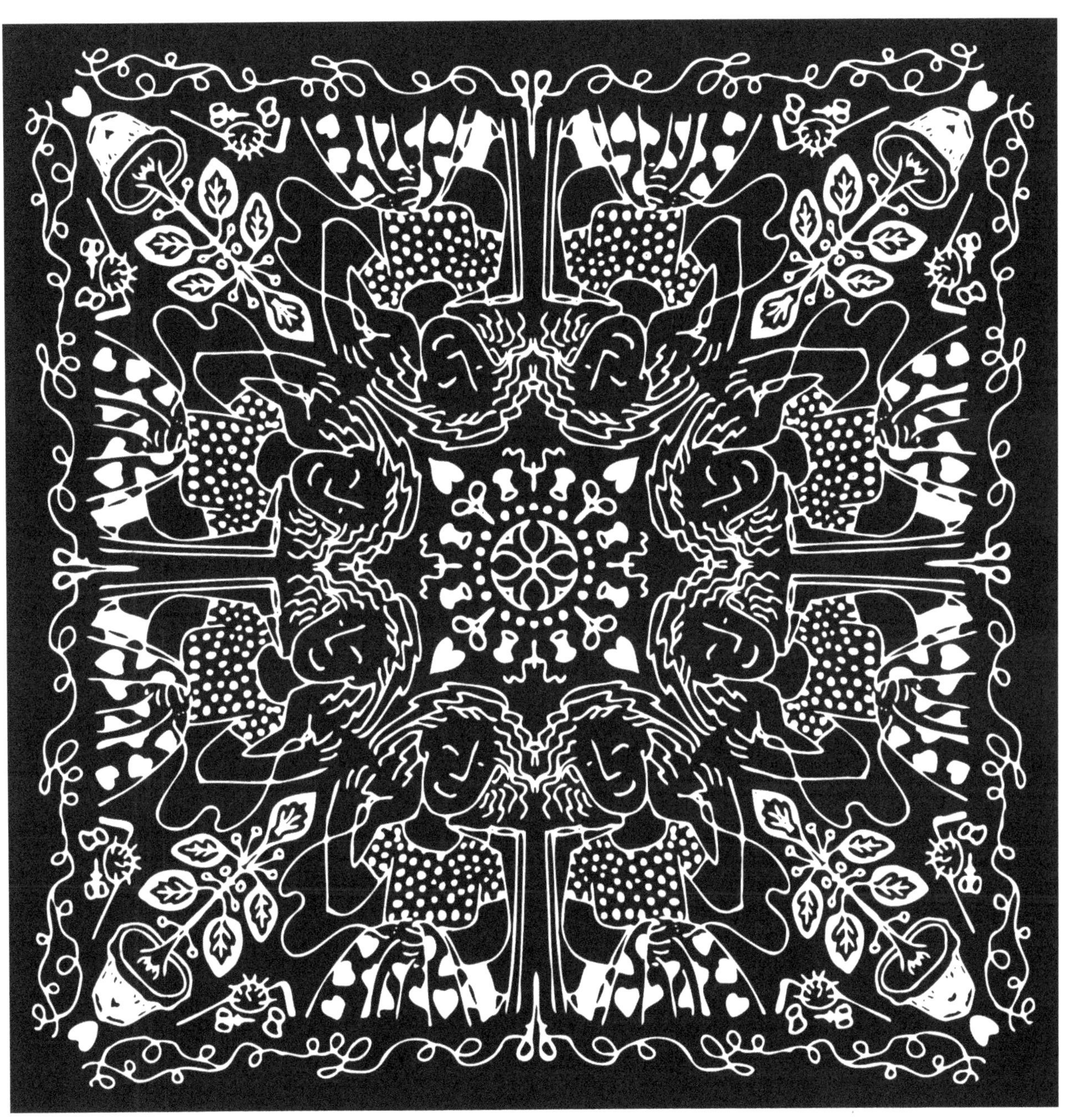

...and Later I'll Work on This Comforter for My Granddaughter

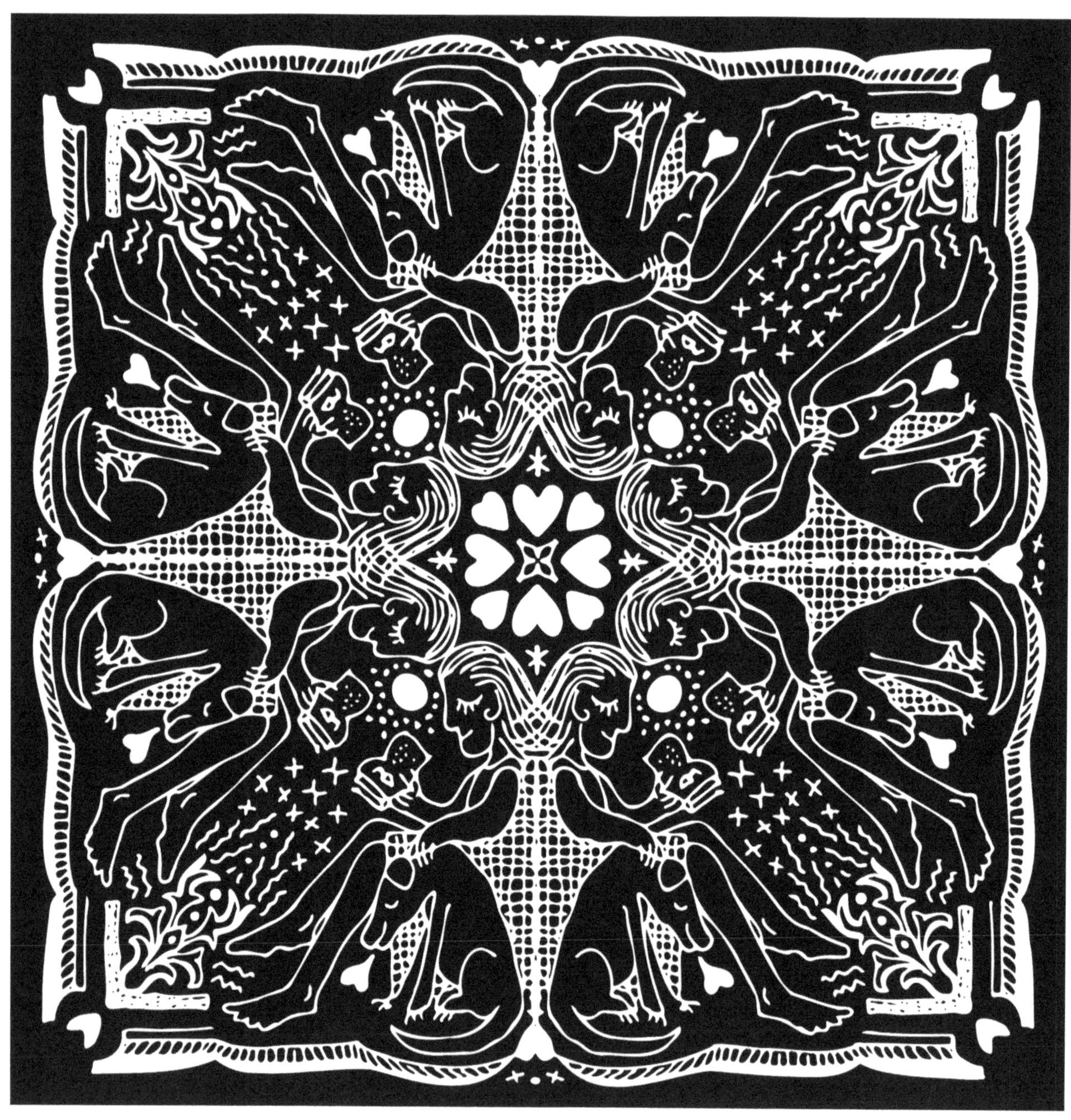

I Love to Sit by the Fire and Read, with Fido by My Side

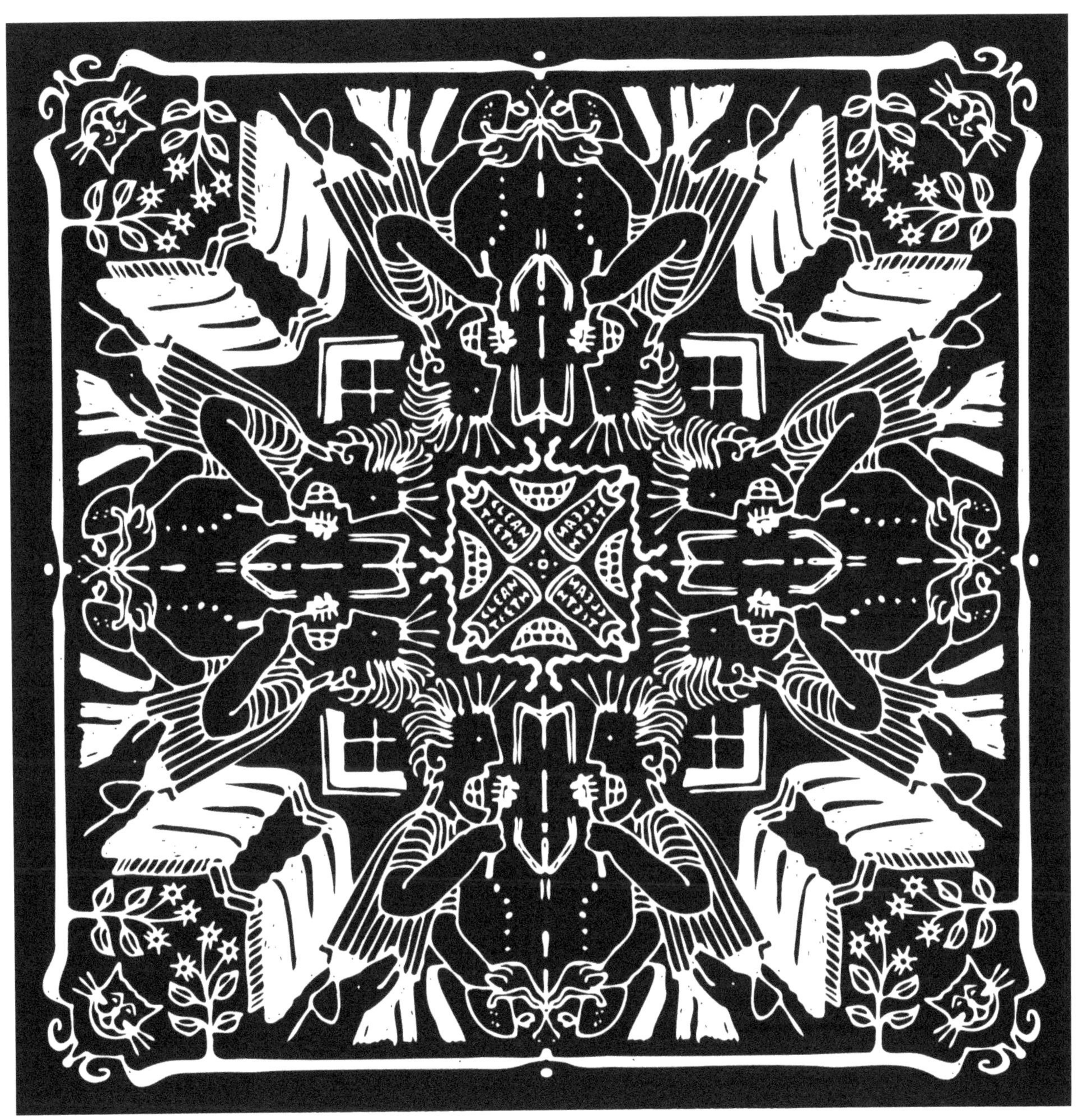

Time to Brush Teeth and Go Nighty-Nite

Story Four

LOVE

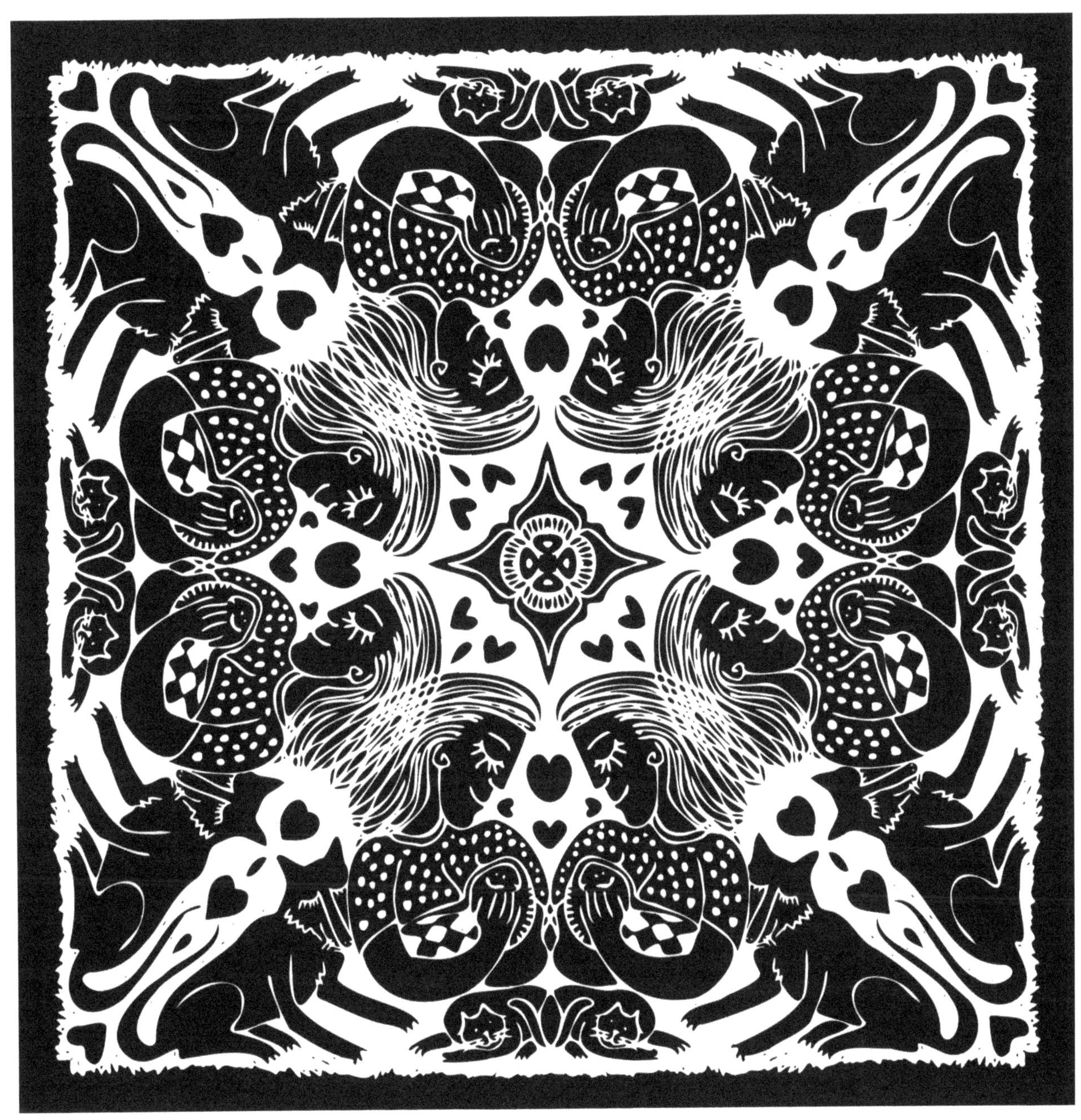

Felix and Fido Love the Newborn

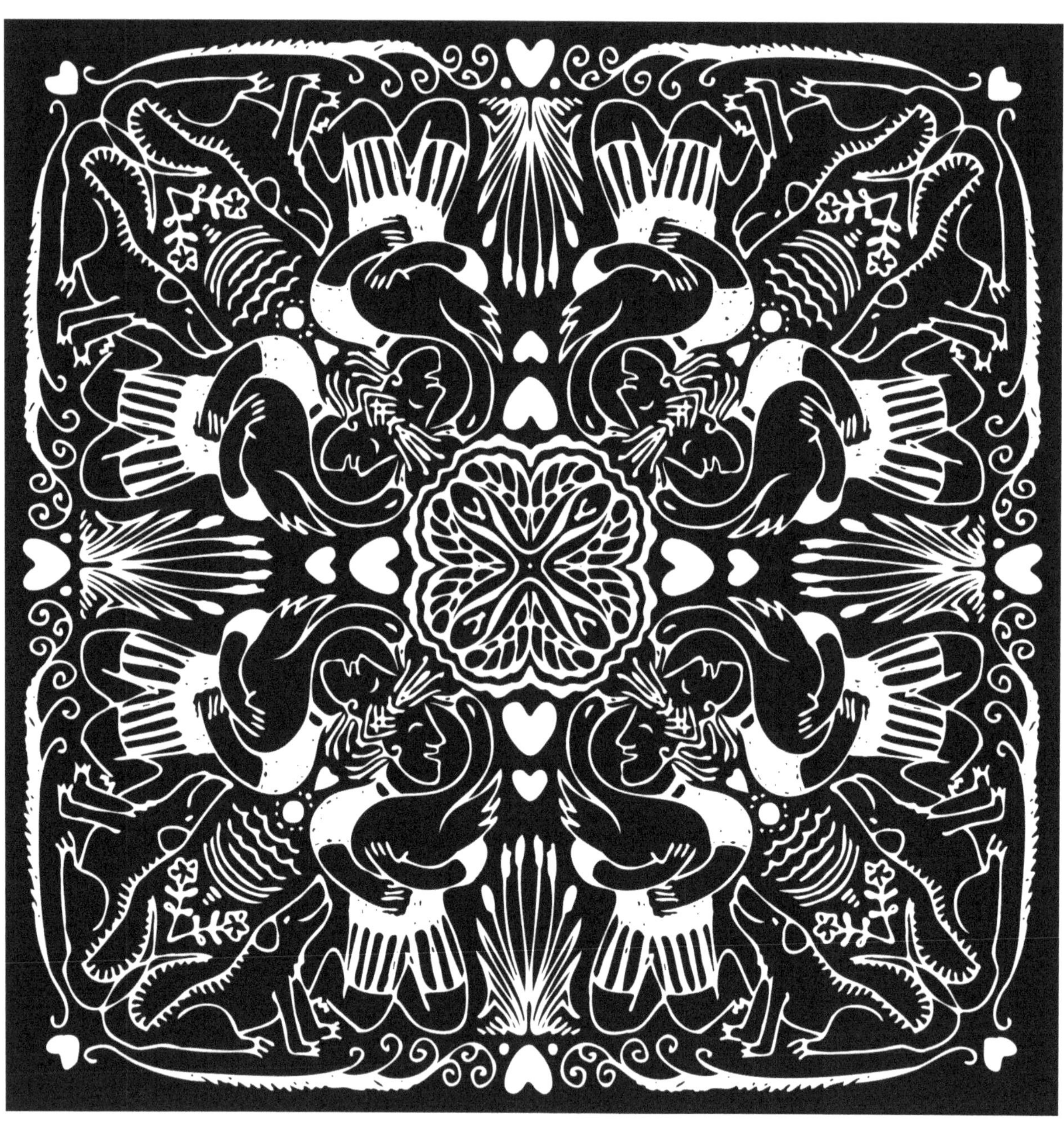

Jimmy and Fido Saved the Swan!

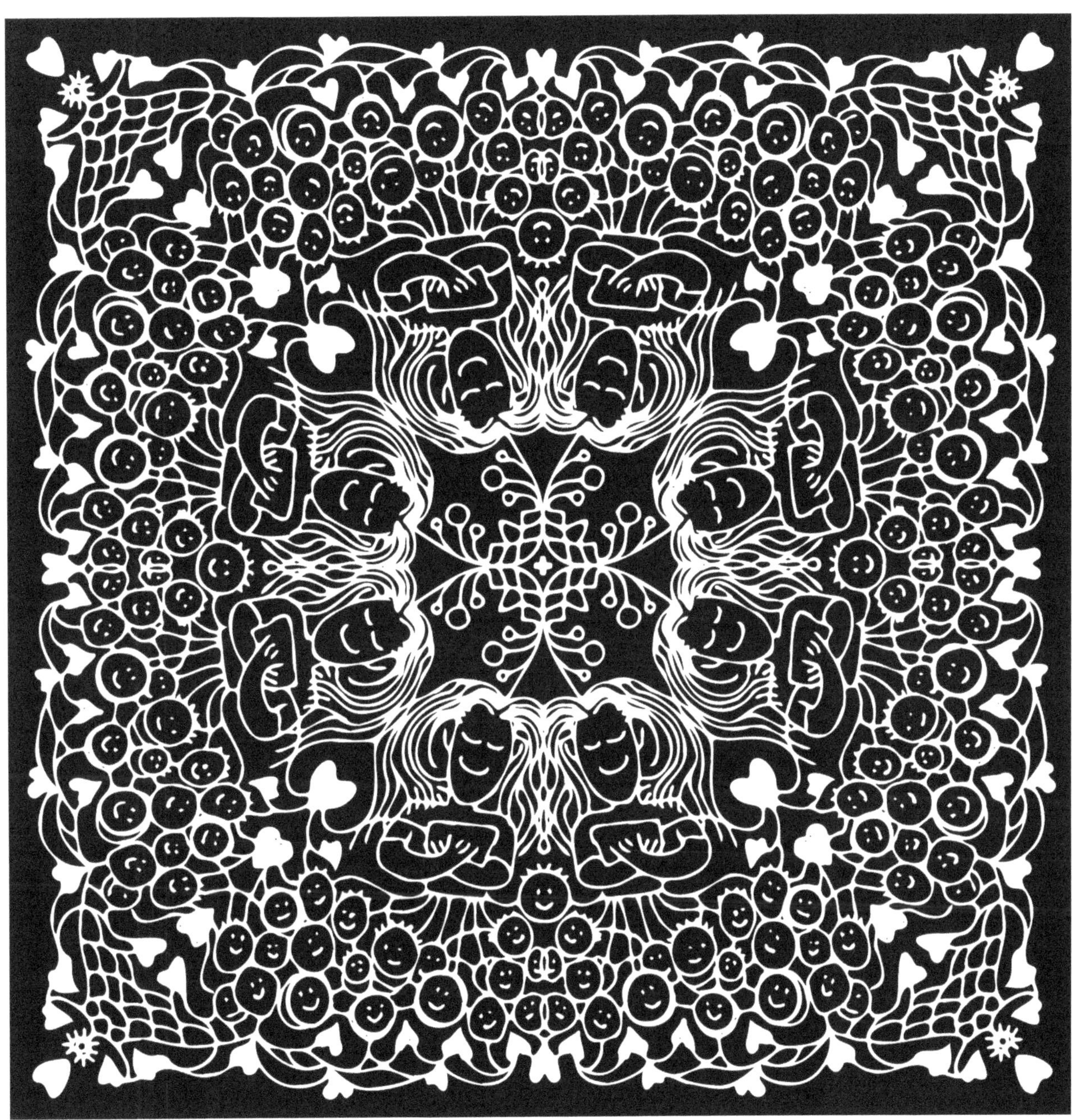

I Love Feeling Connected by the Internet

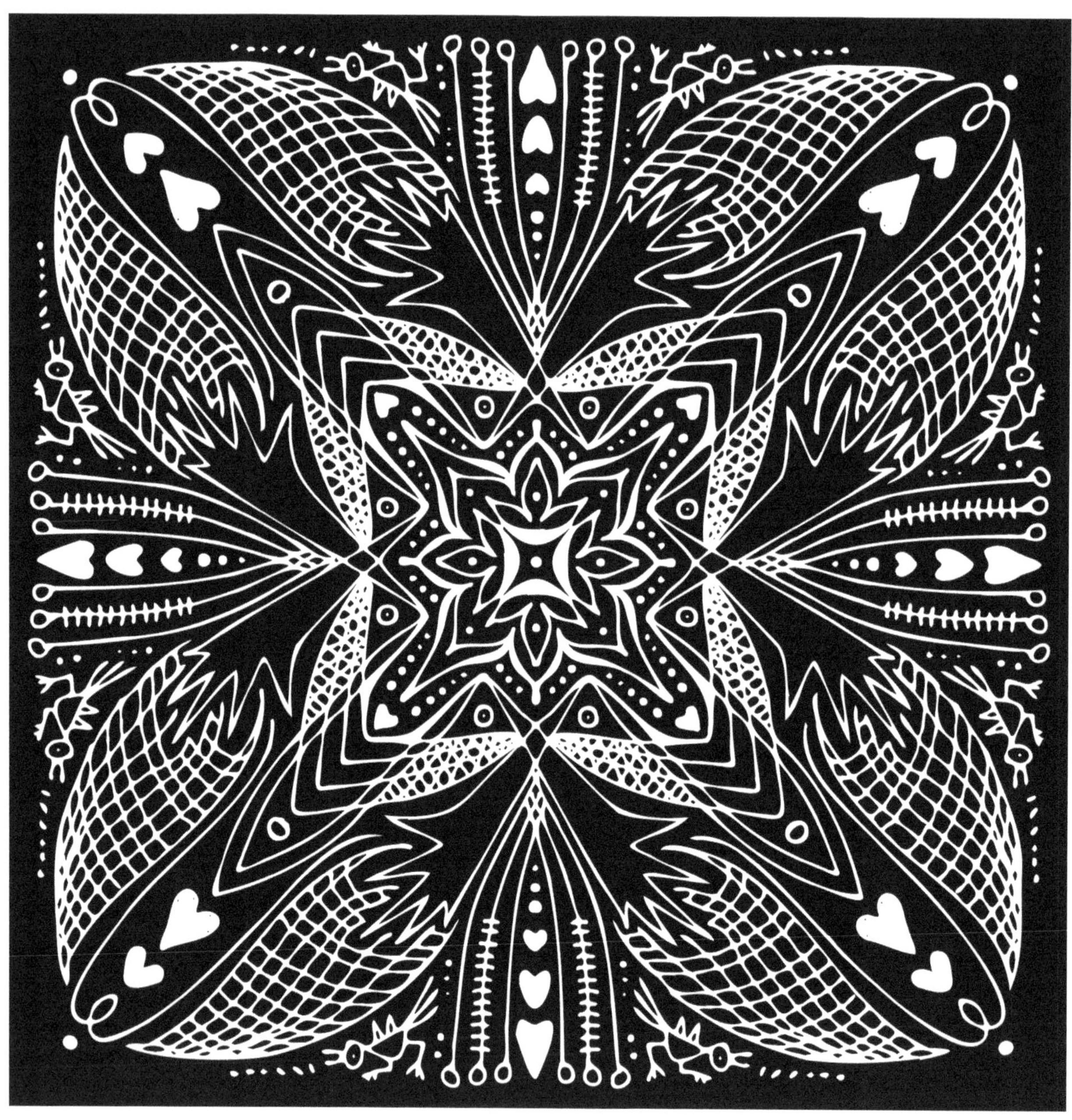

Cast Your Net of Love

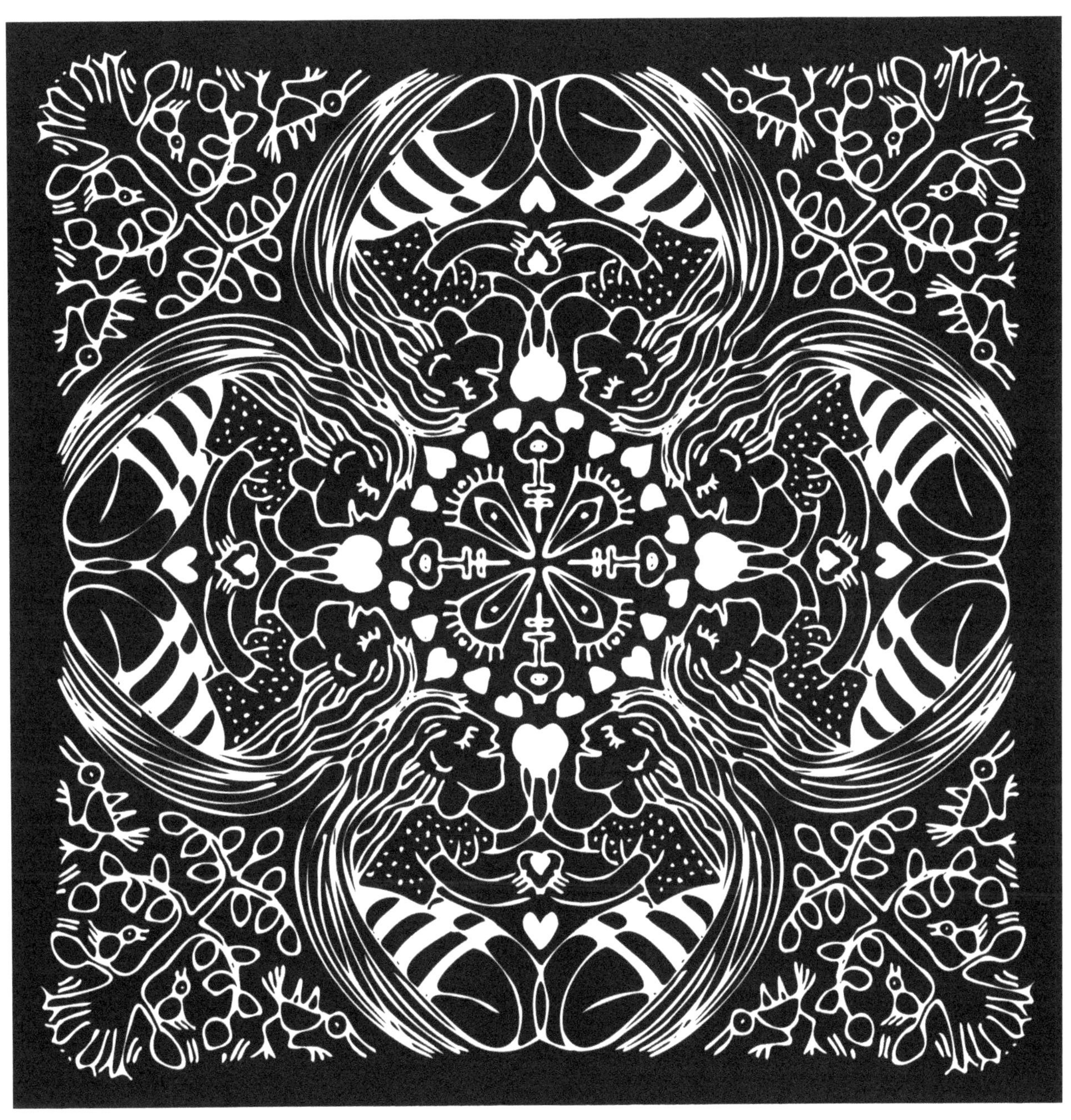

Here's the Key to My Heart

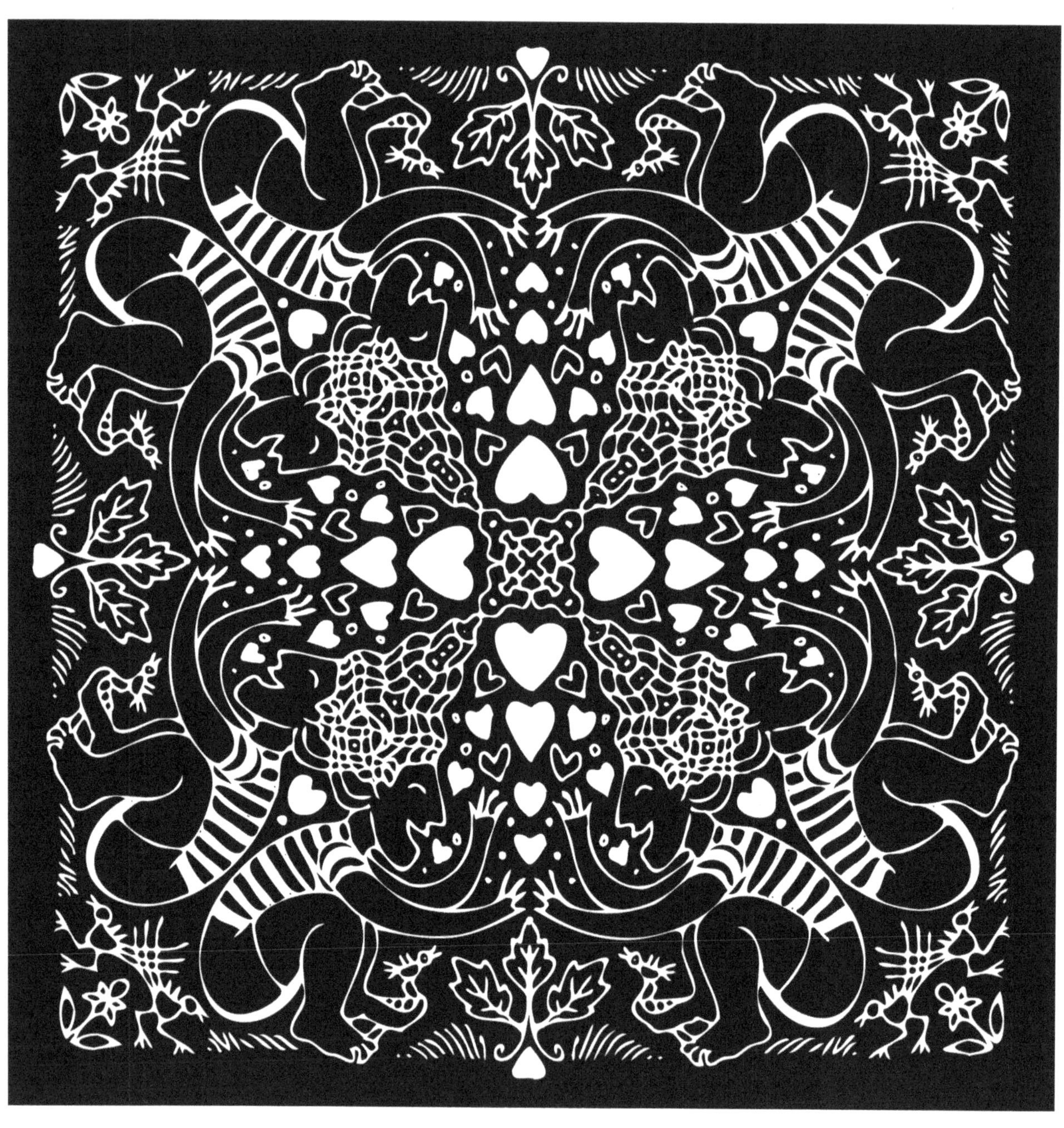

Juggling Love

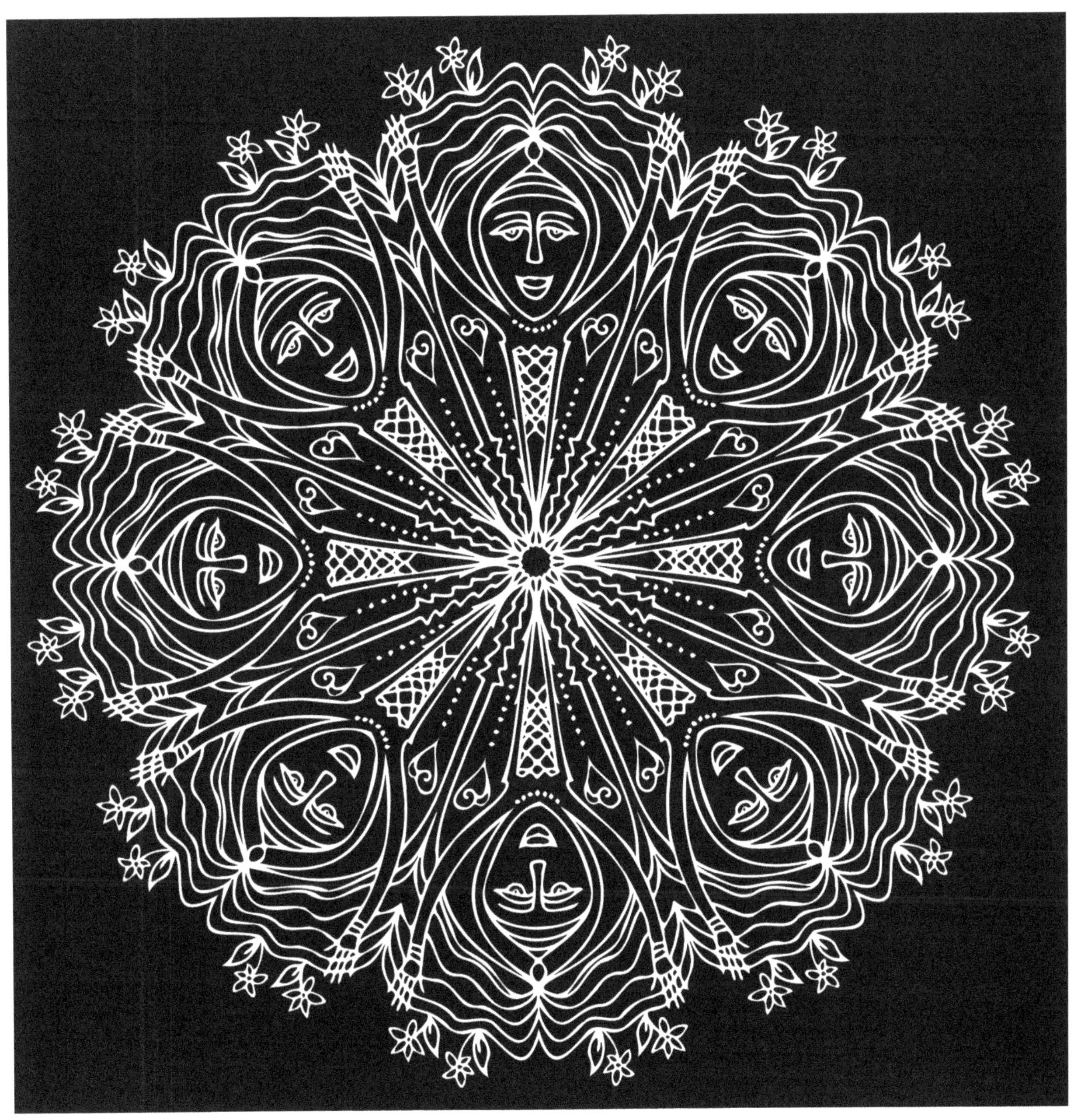

They Put A Love Spell On Me!

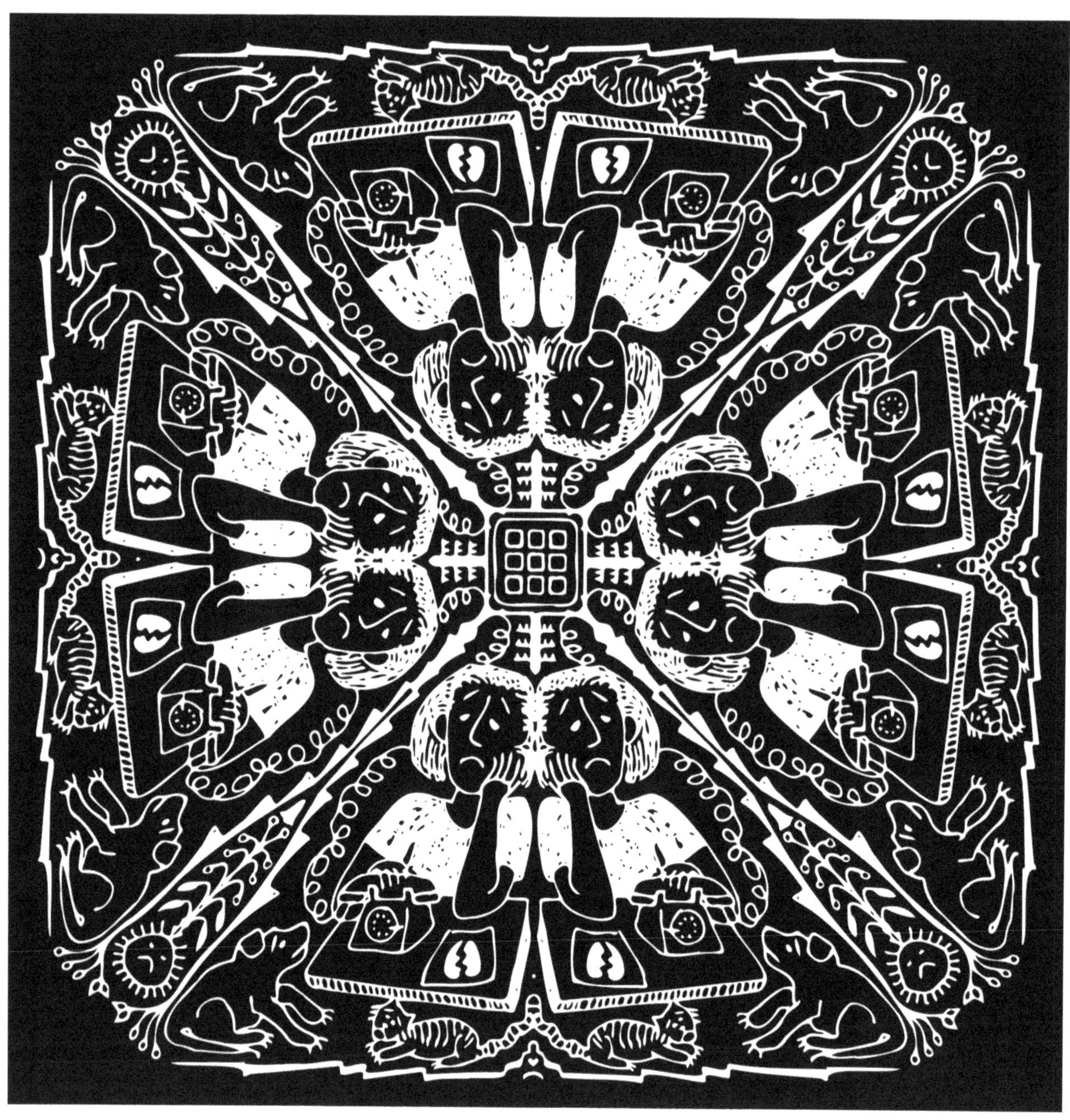

Waiting and Waiting for Your Call

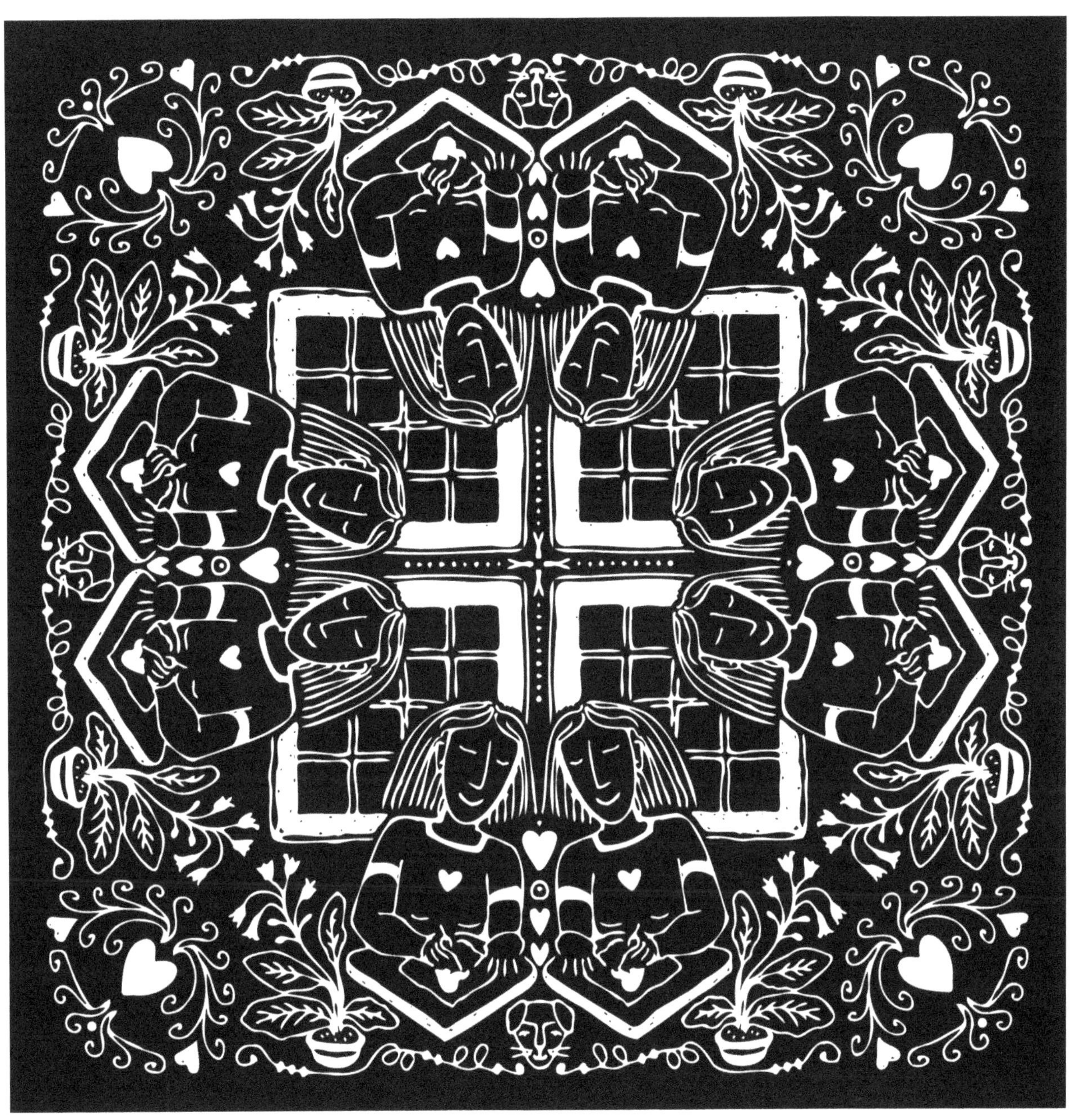

I Love It that You Love Me!

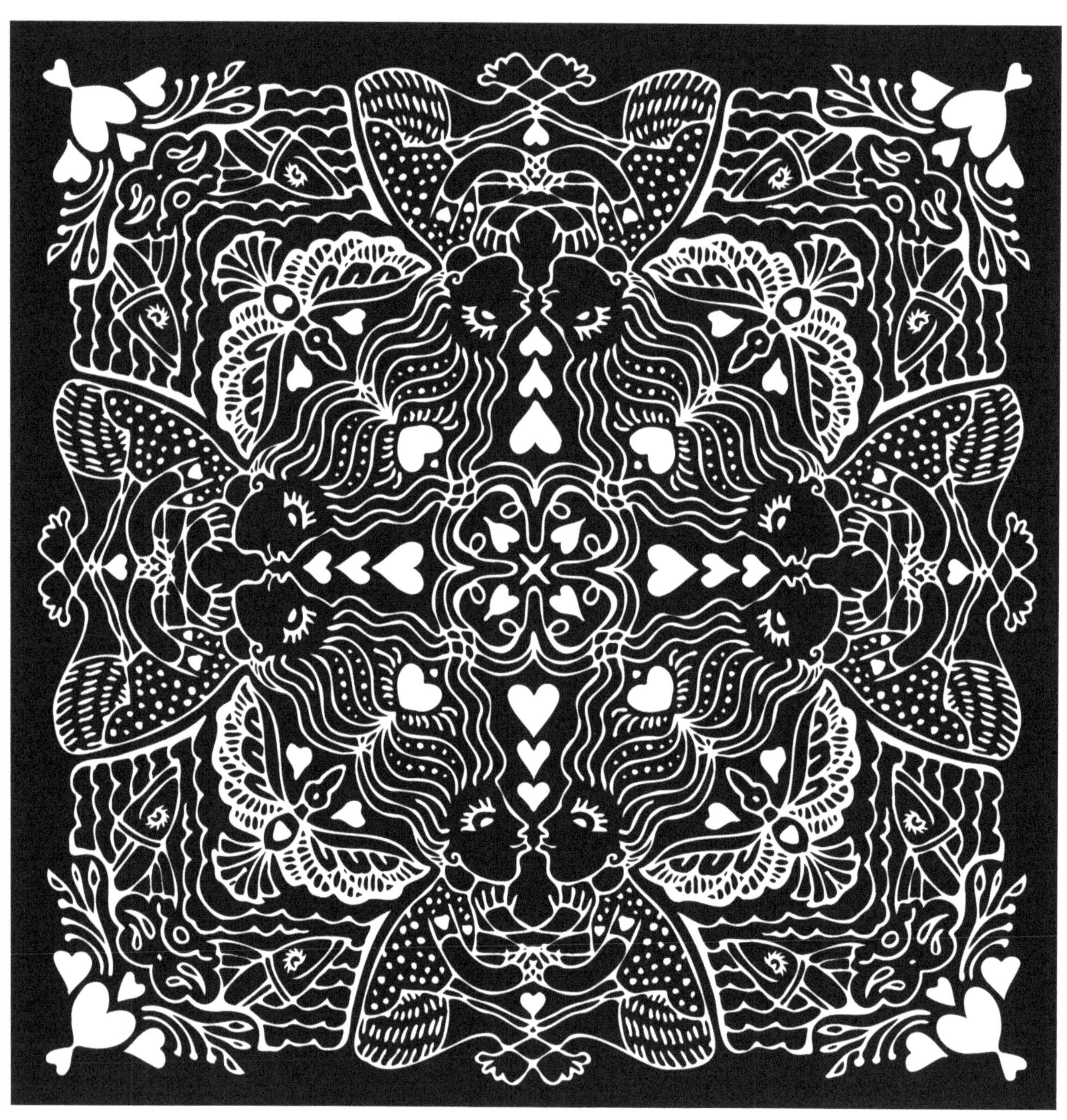

Love Birds

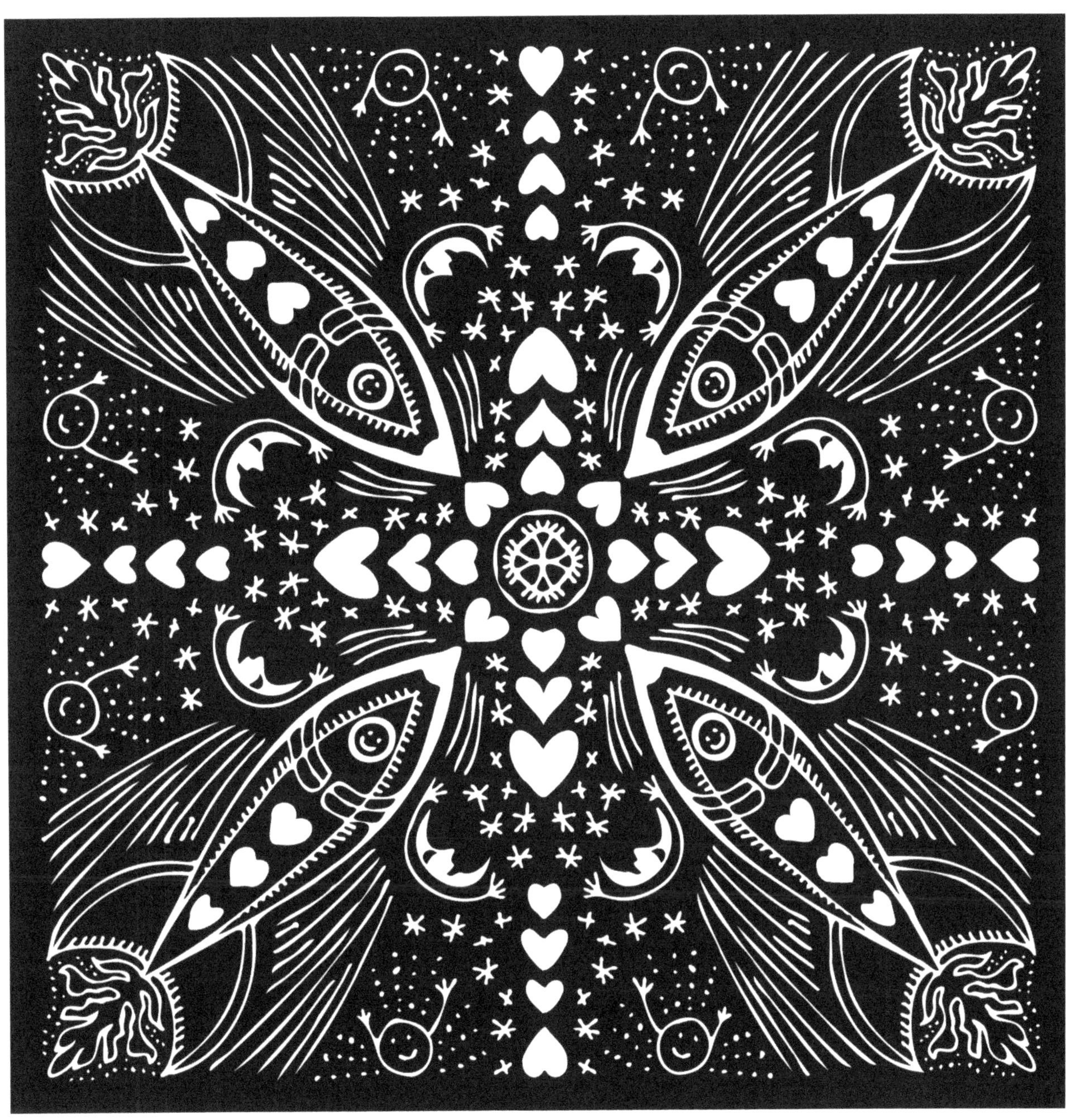

I'm A Rocket for Your Love, Baby!

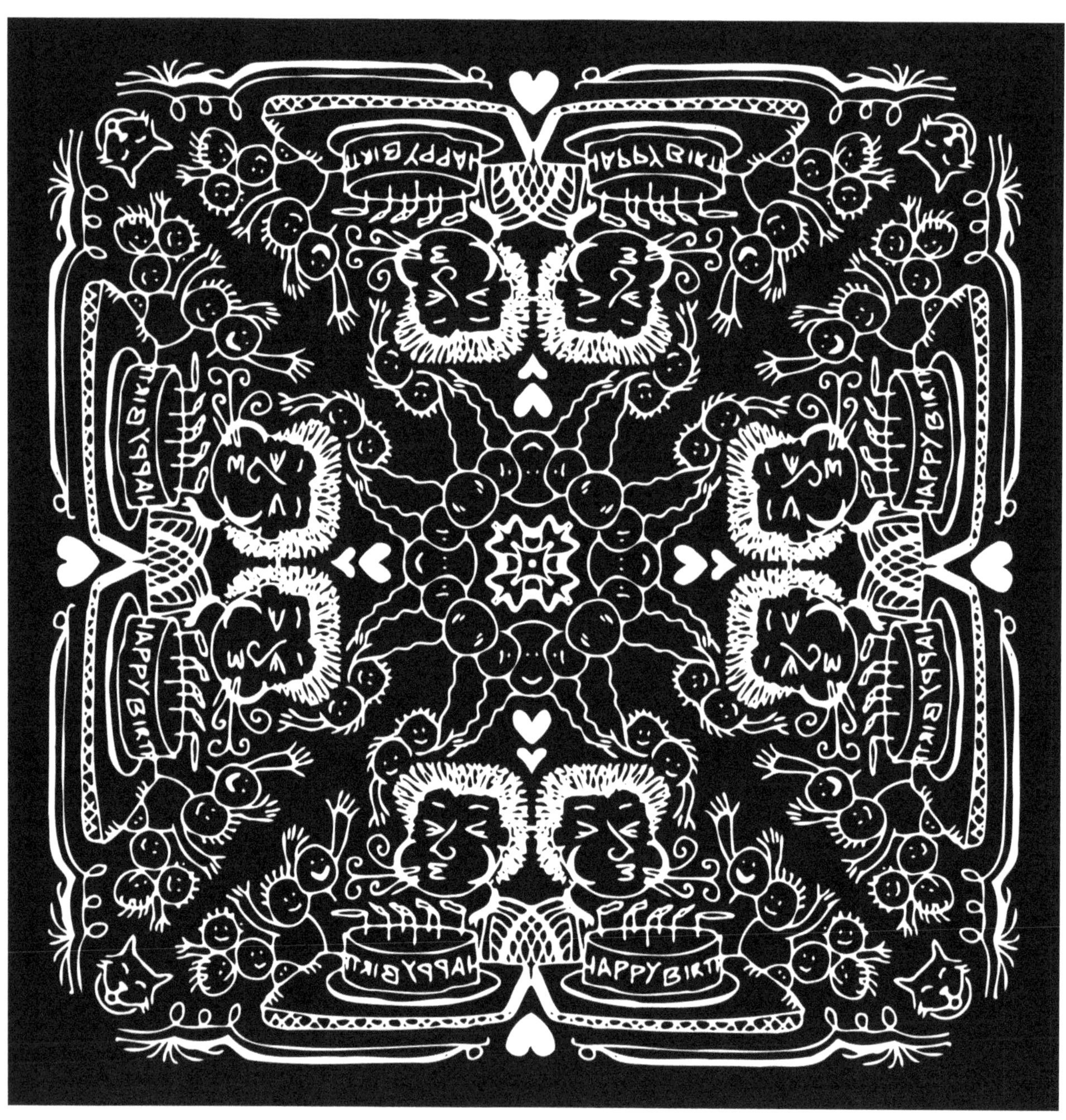

Happy Birthday toooooo Yoooouuuu!!!

Story Five

MUSIC

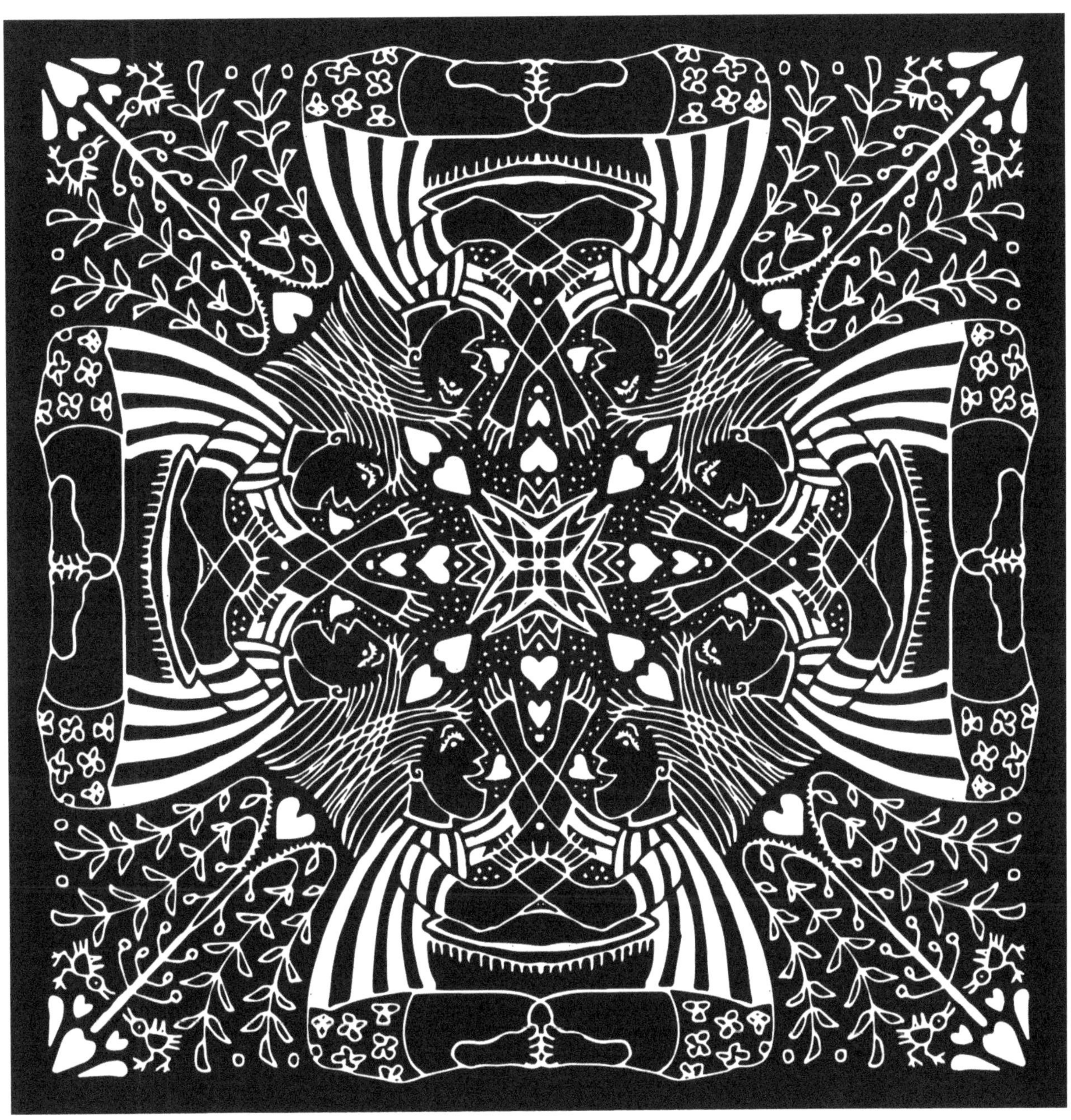

Drumming the Planet's Heart Beat

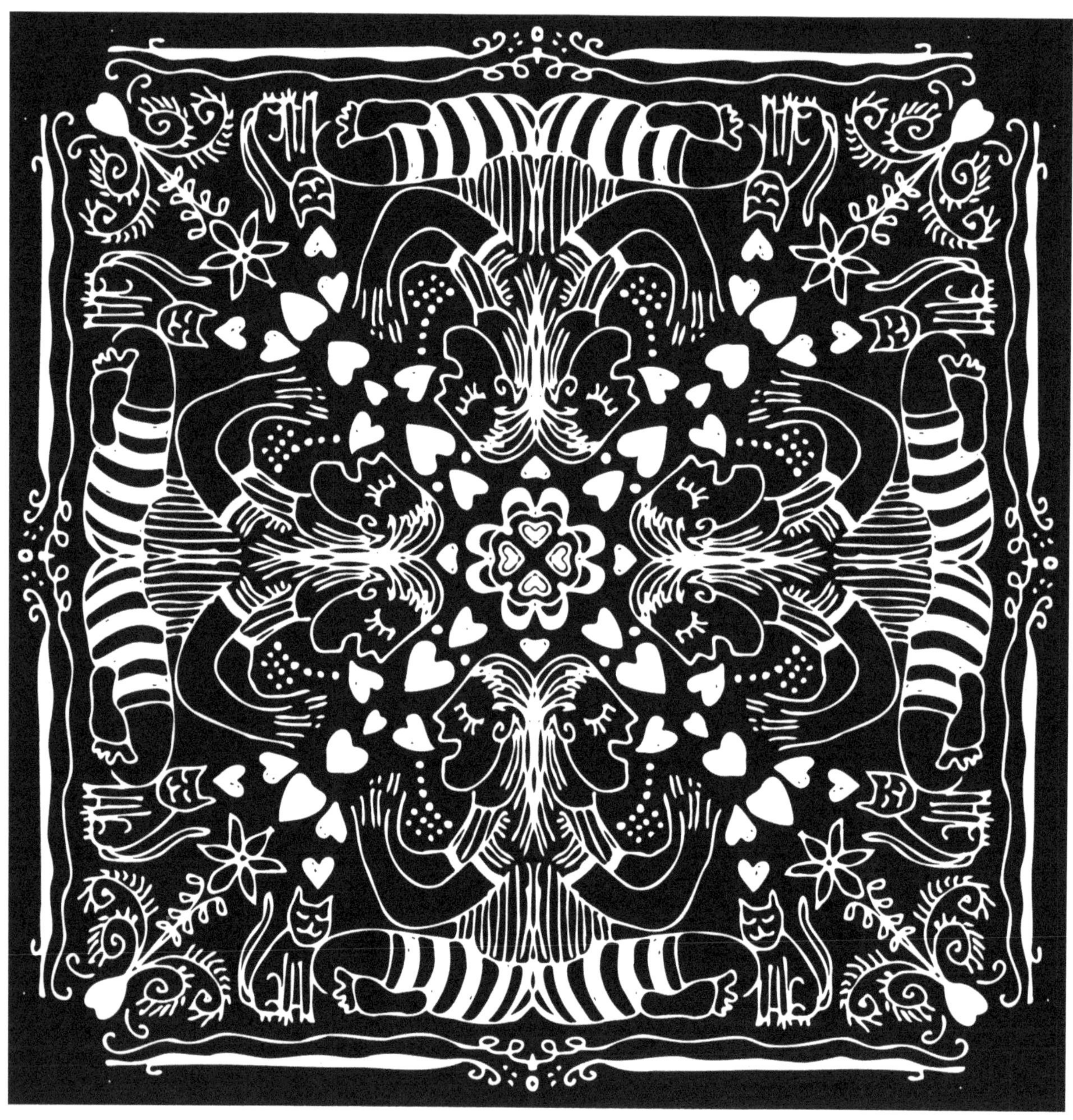

Even Felix Likes Chanting for Harmony

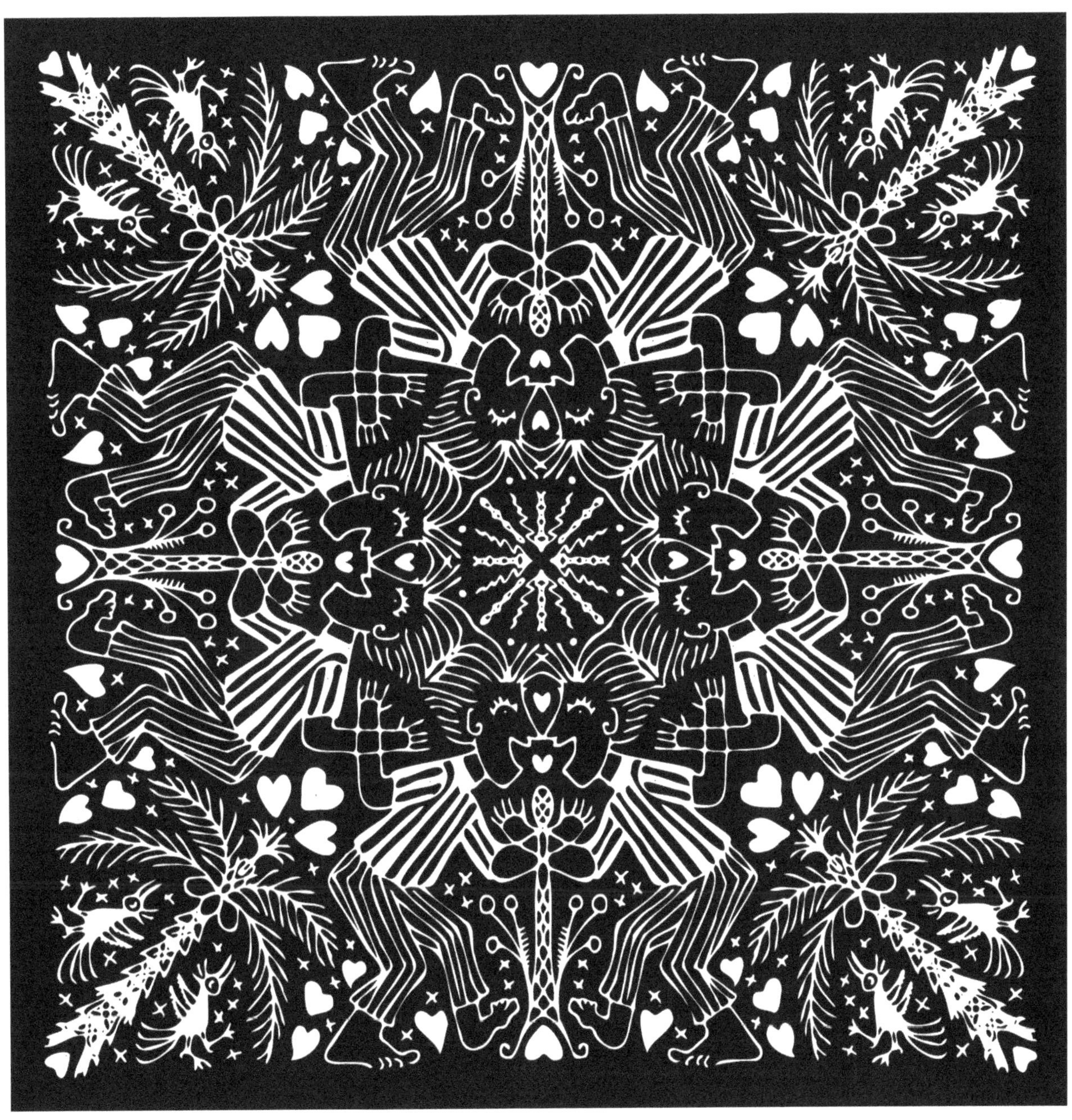

Sing and Dance for Love

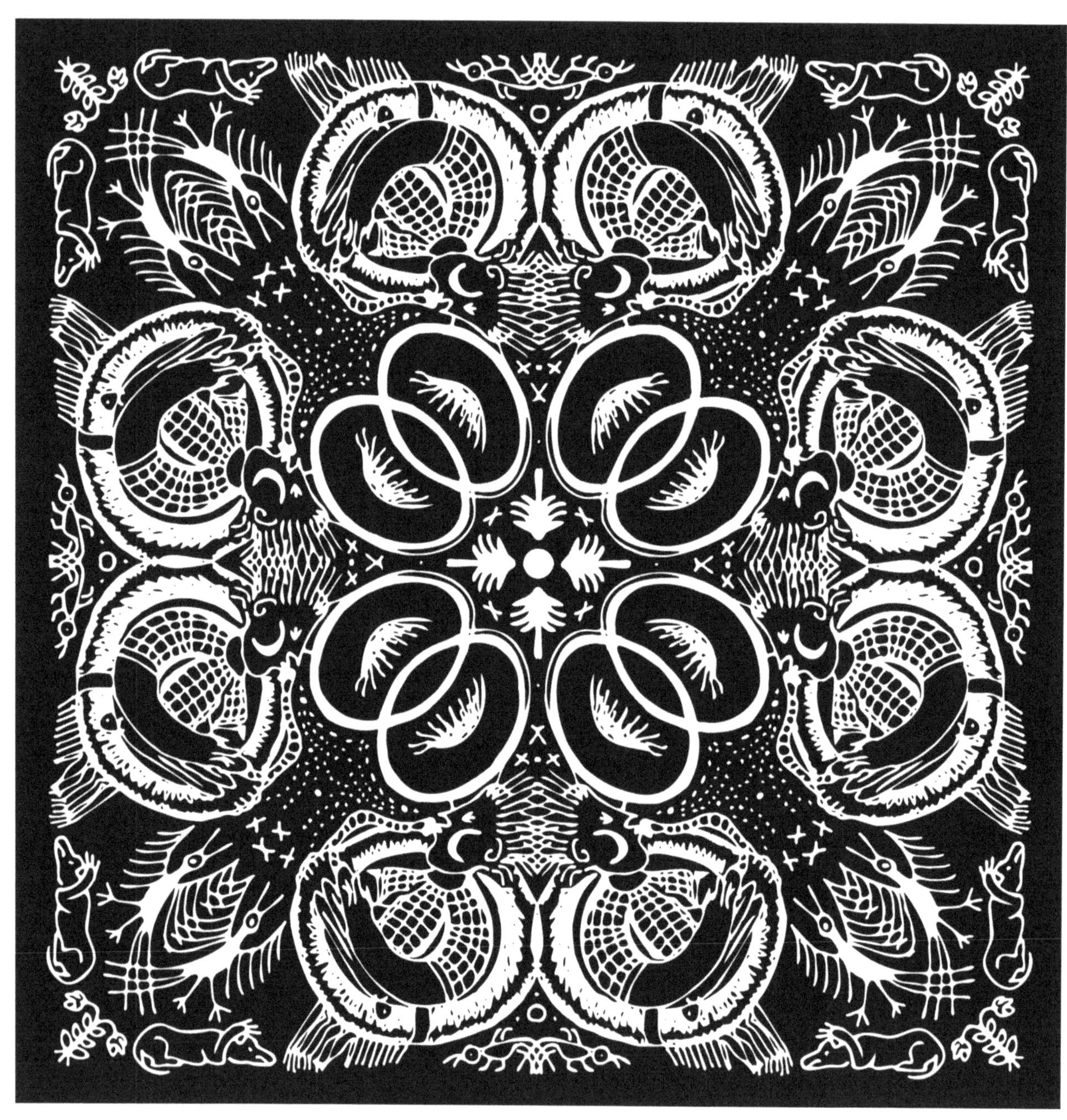

I'd Never Heard of A Sousaphone Before

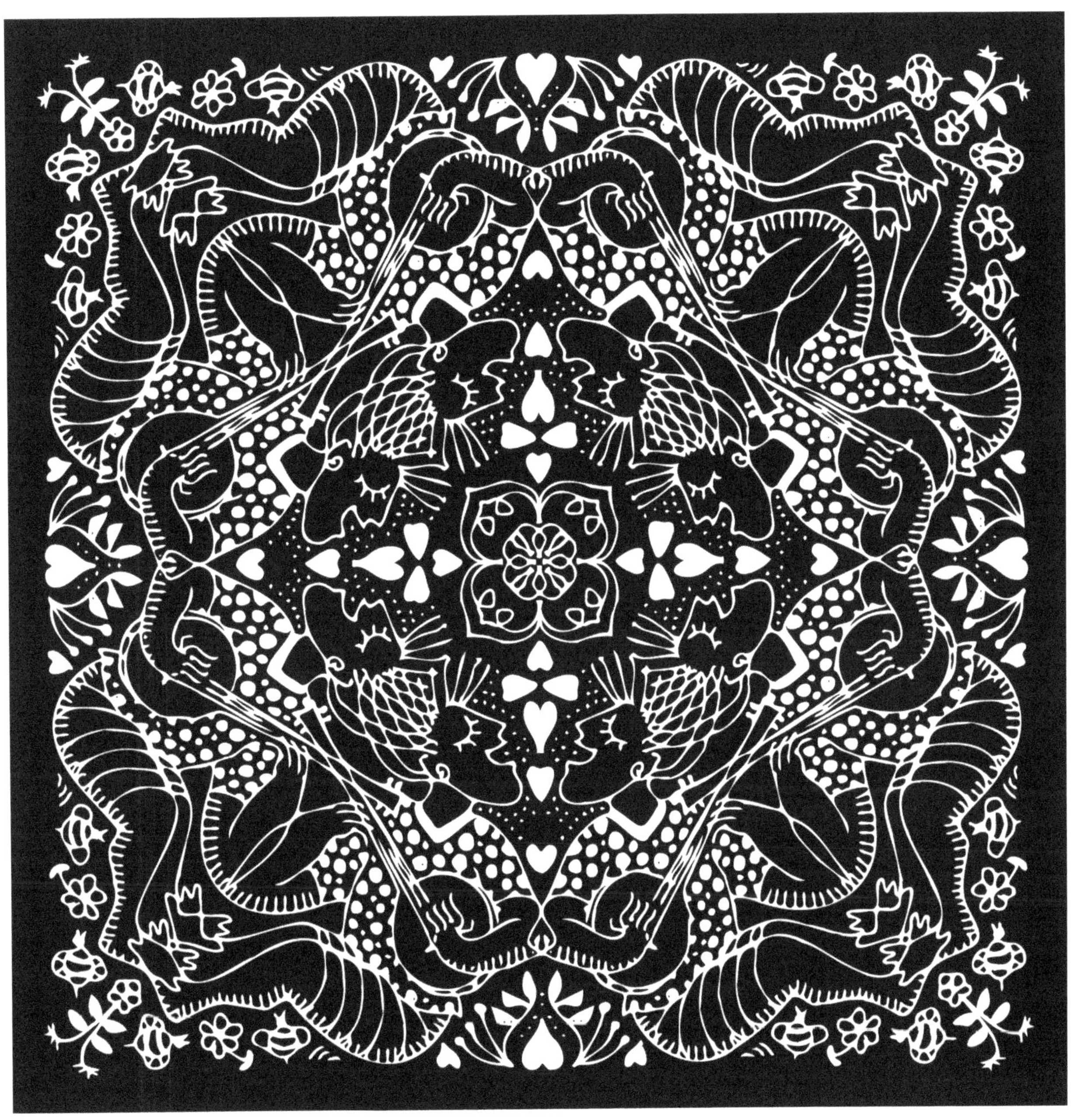

Bees, Banjos and Bluegrass

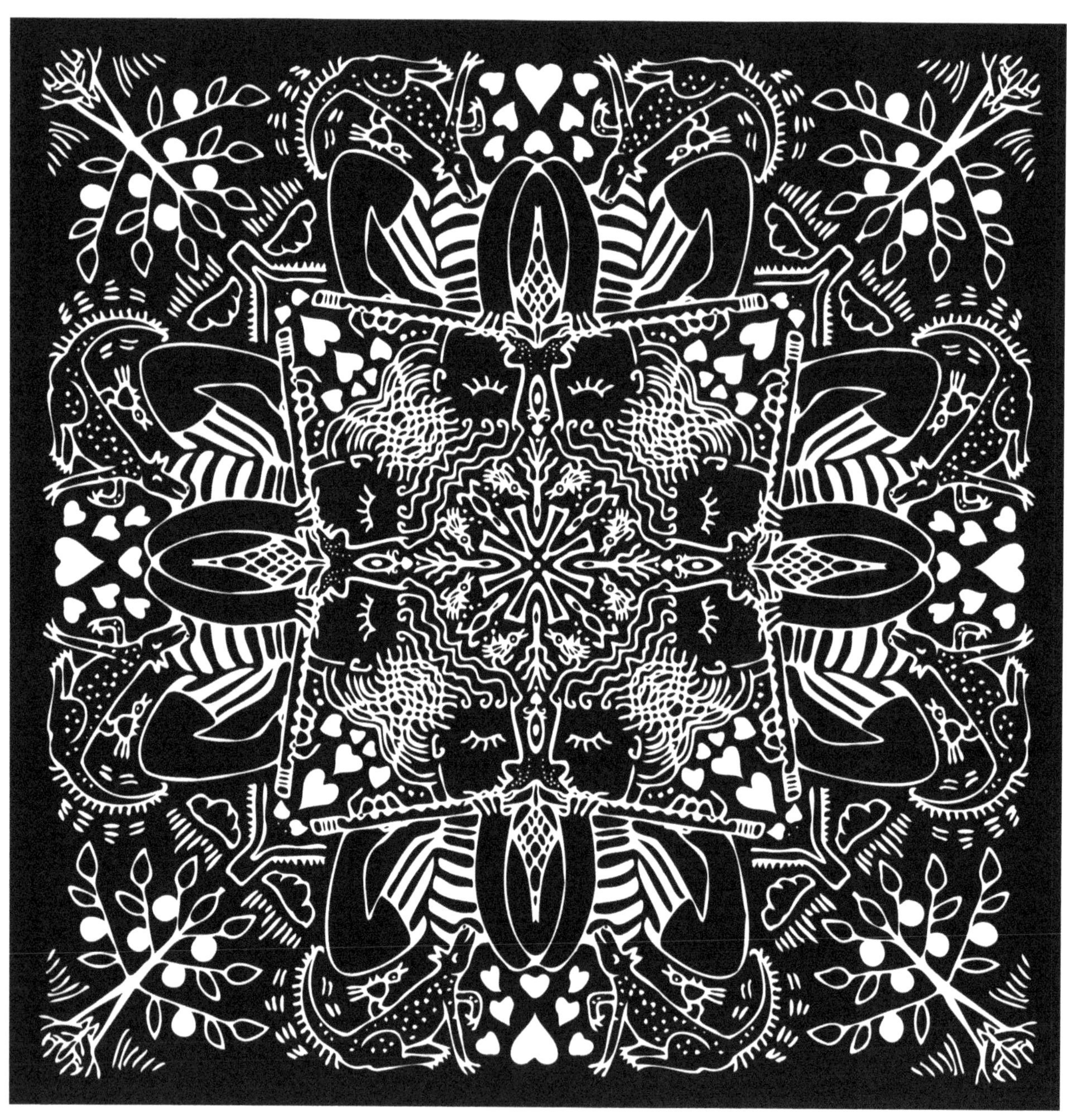

Flutes Sometimes Sound Like Birds, or Rain On the Leaves

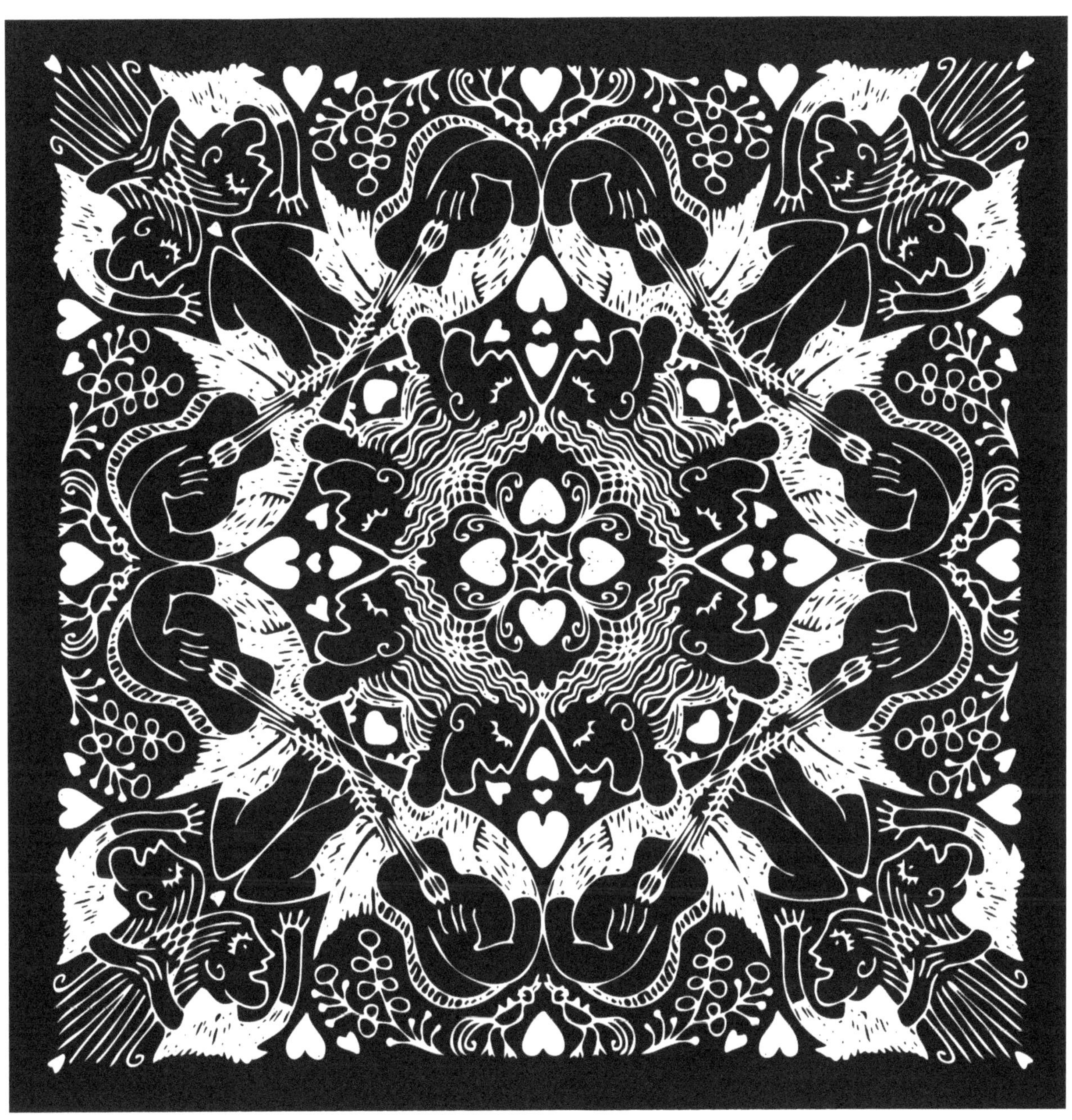

Everyone Dances When Jimmy Plays His Guitar

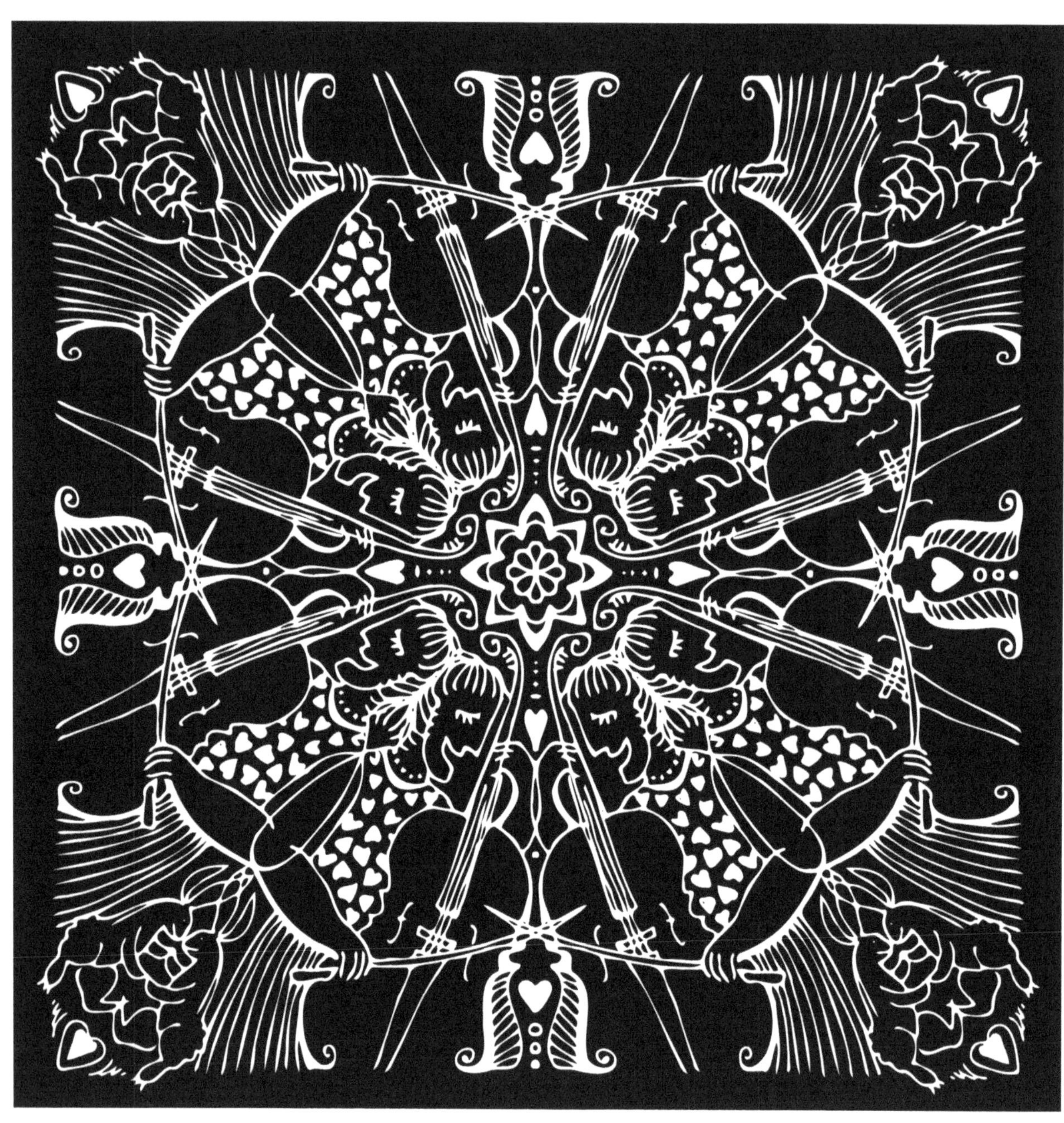

Viola Music Can Make Your Soul Shiver

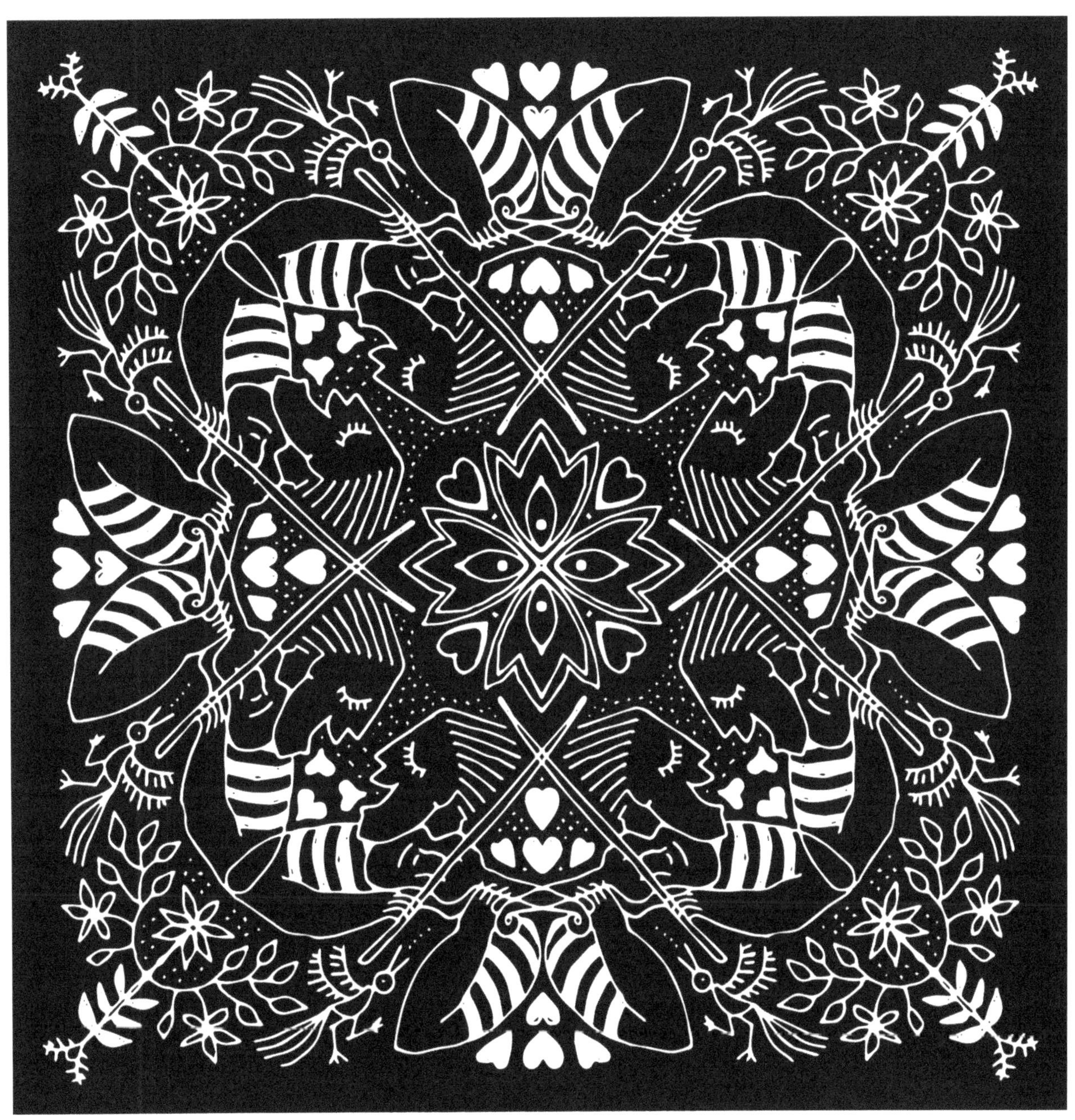

Is It A Violin or A Fiddle?

Story Six

SPORTS FUN

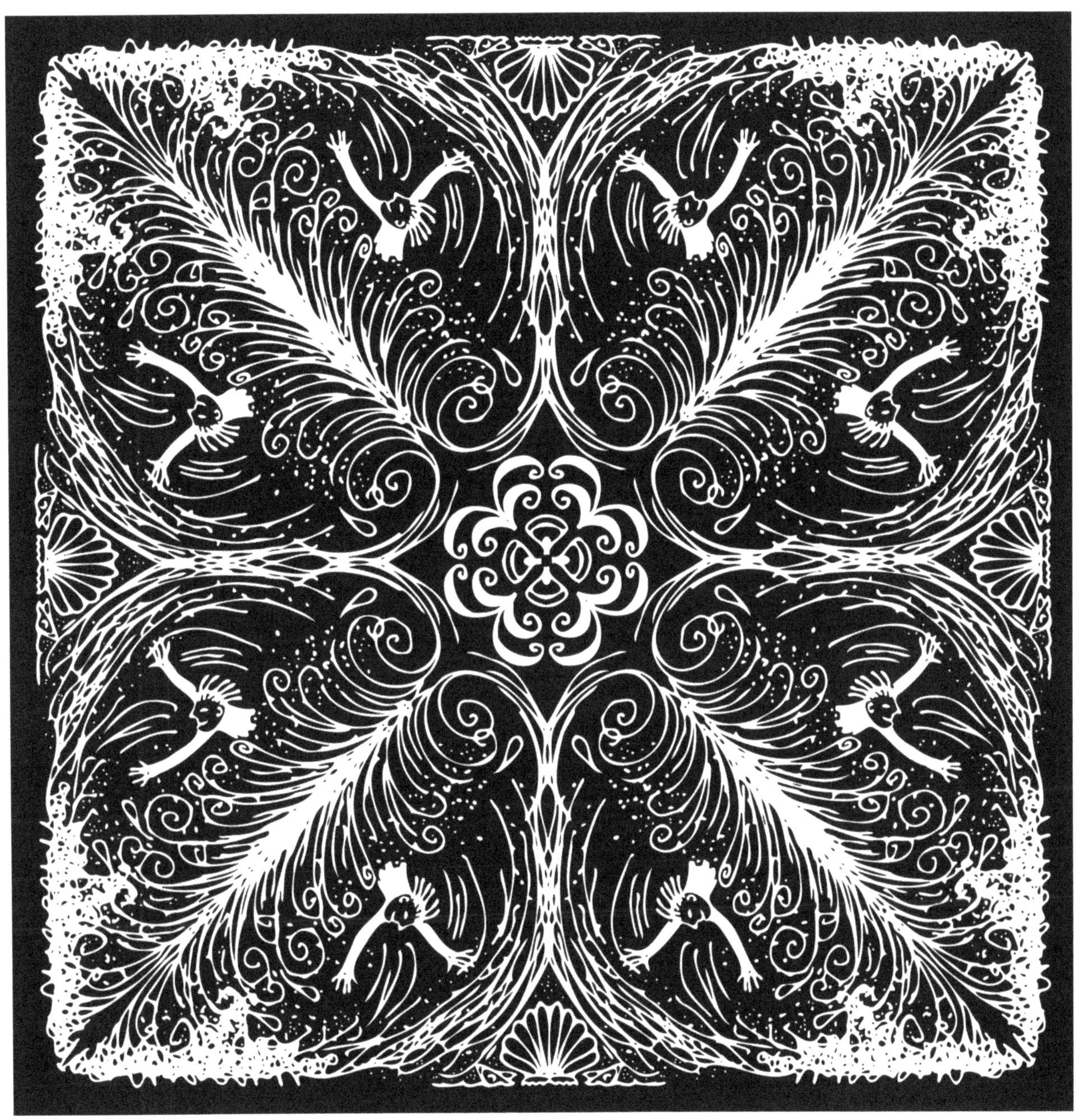

The Big Wave

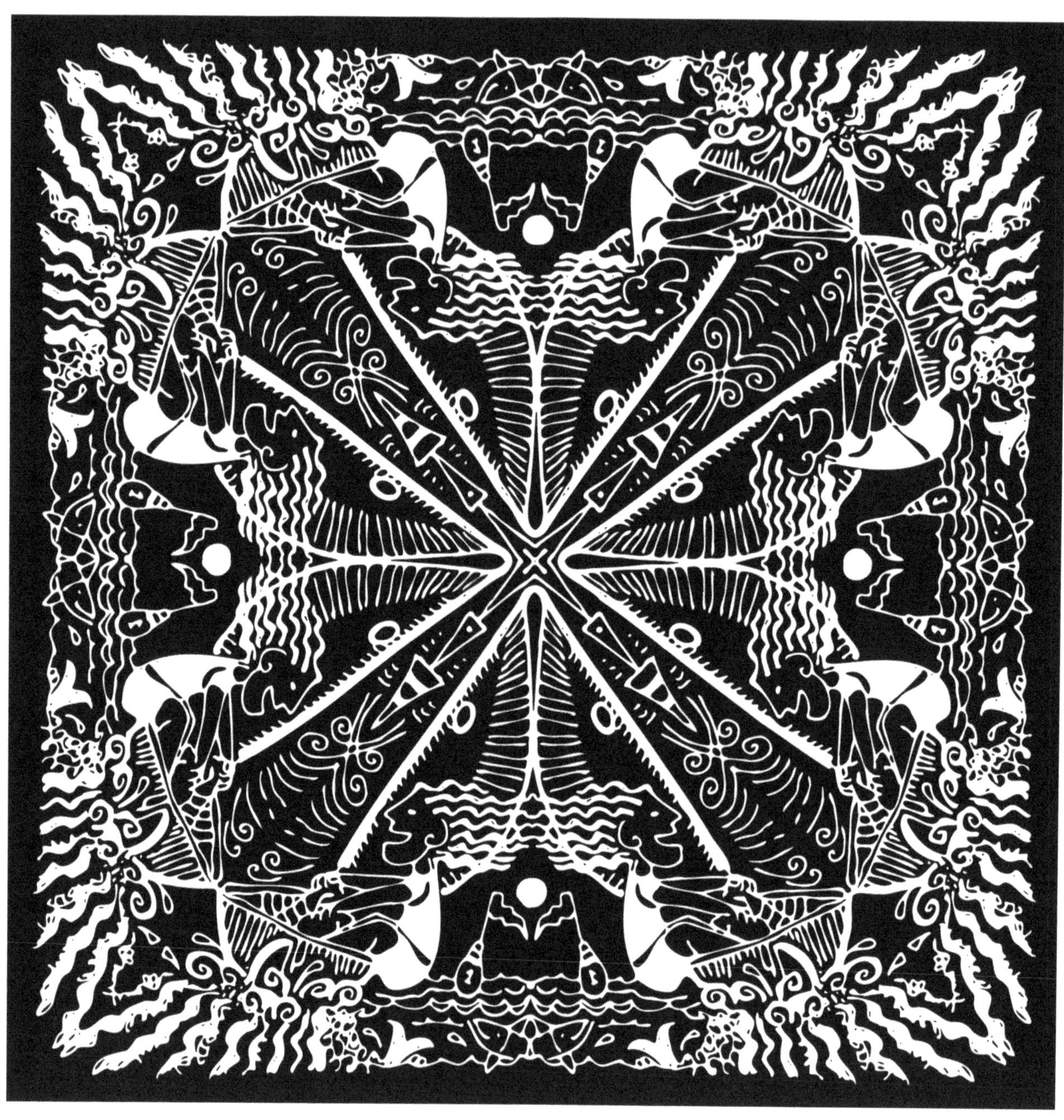

Sailing Close to the Wind

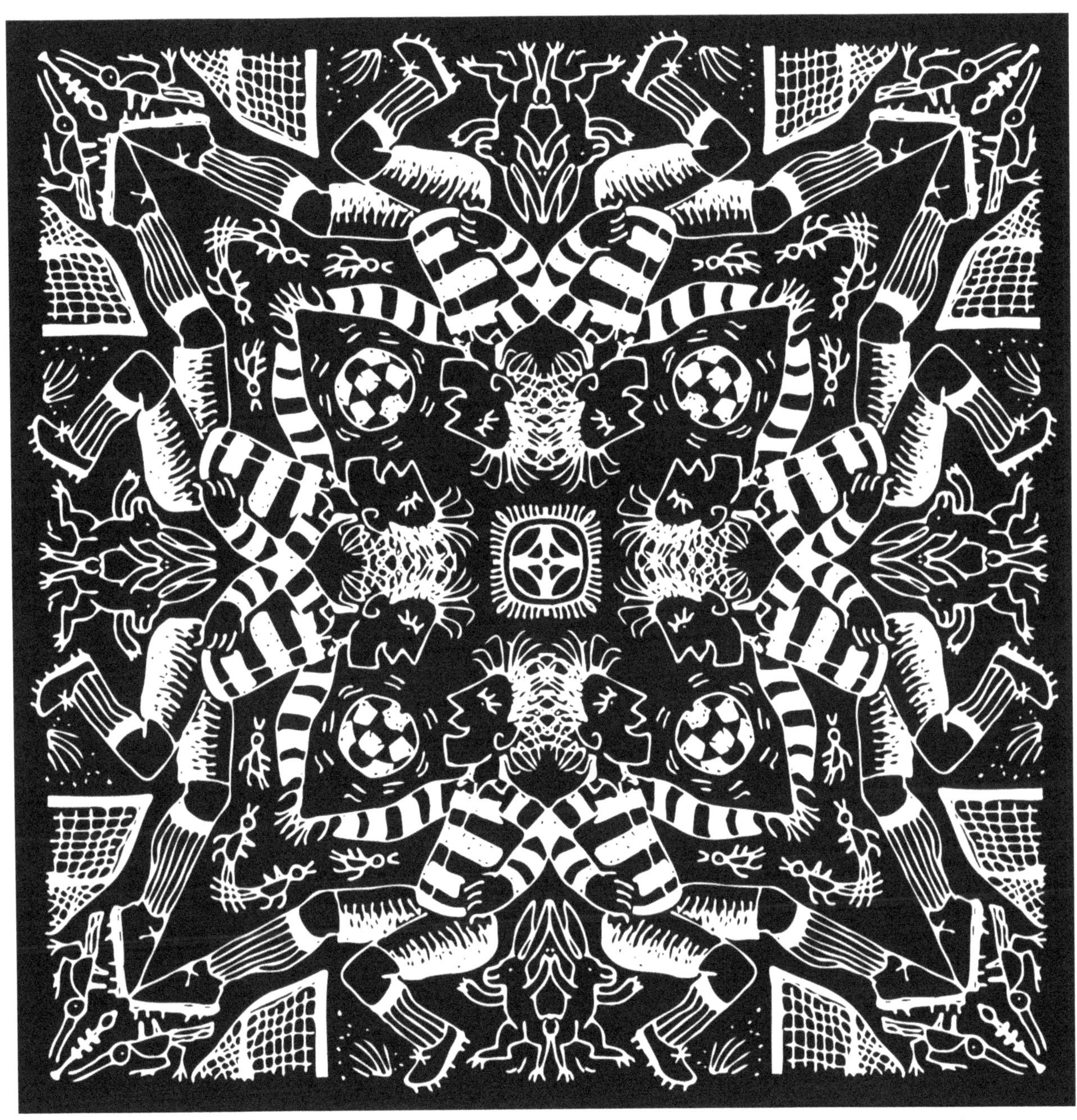

Bunnies, Birdies and Soccer Goals

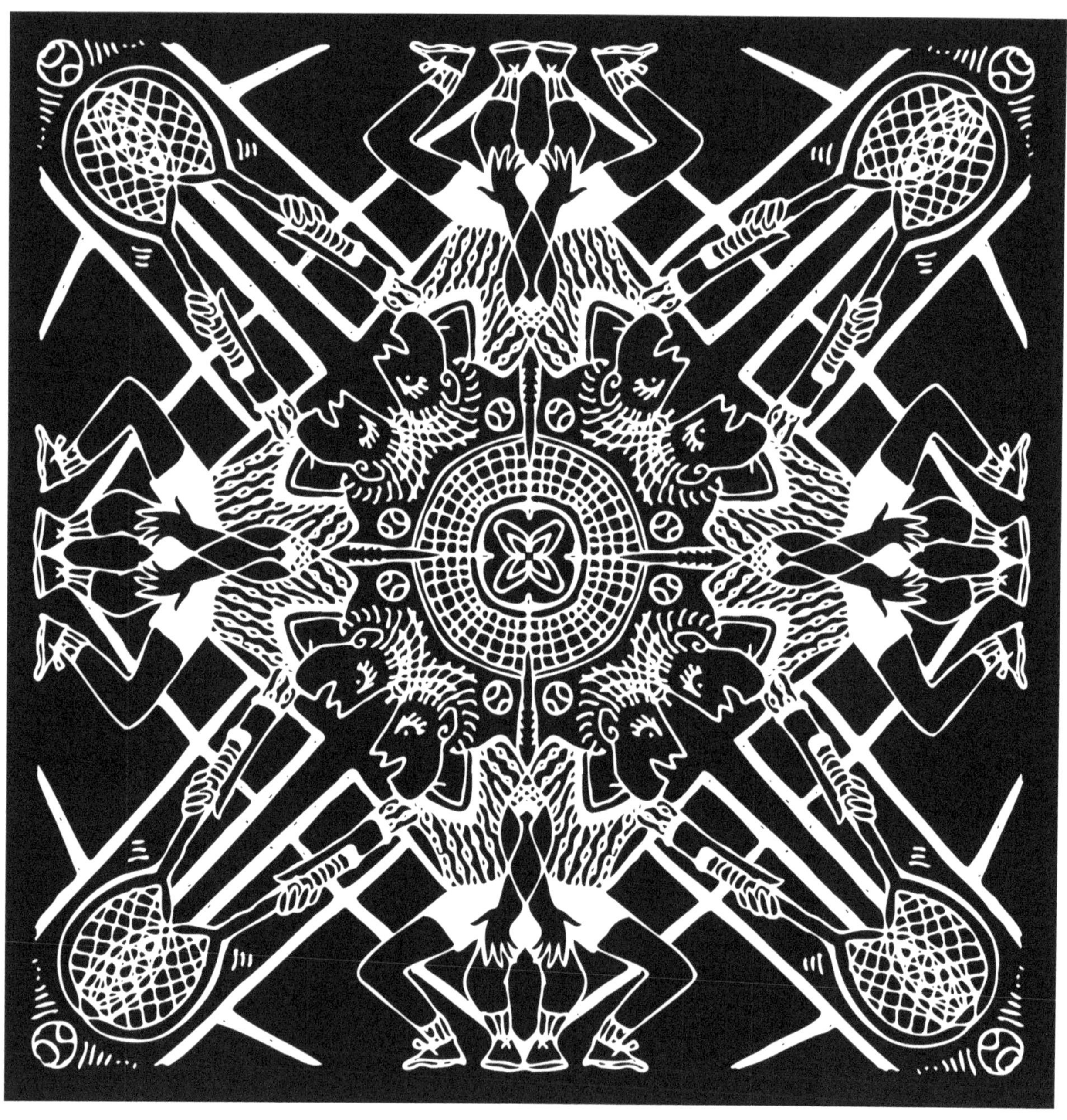

And the Score Is Love-One

Story Seven

CRITTERS, FISH and BIRDIES

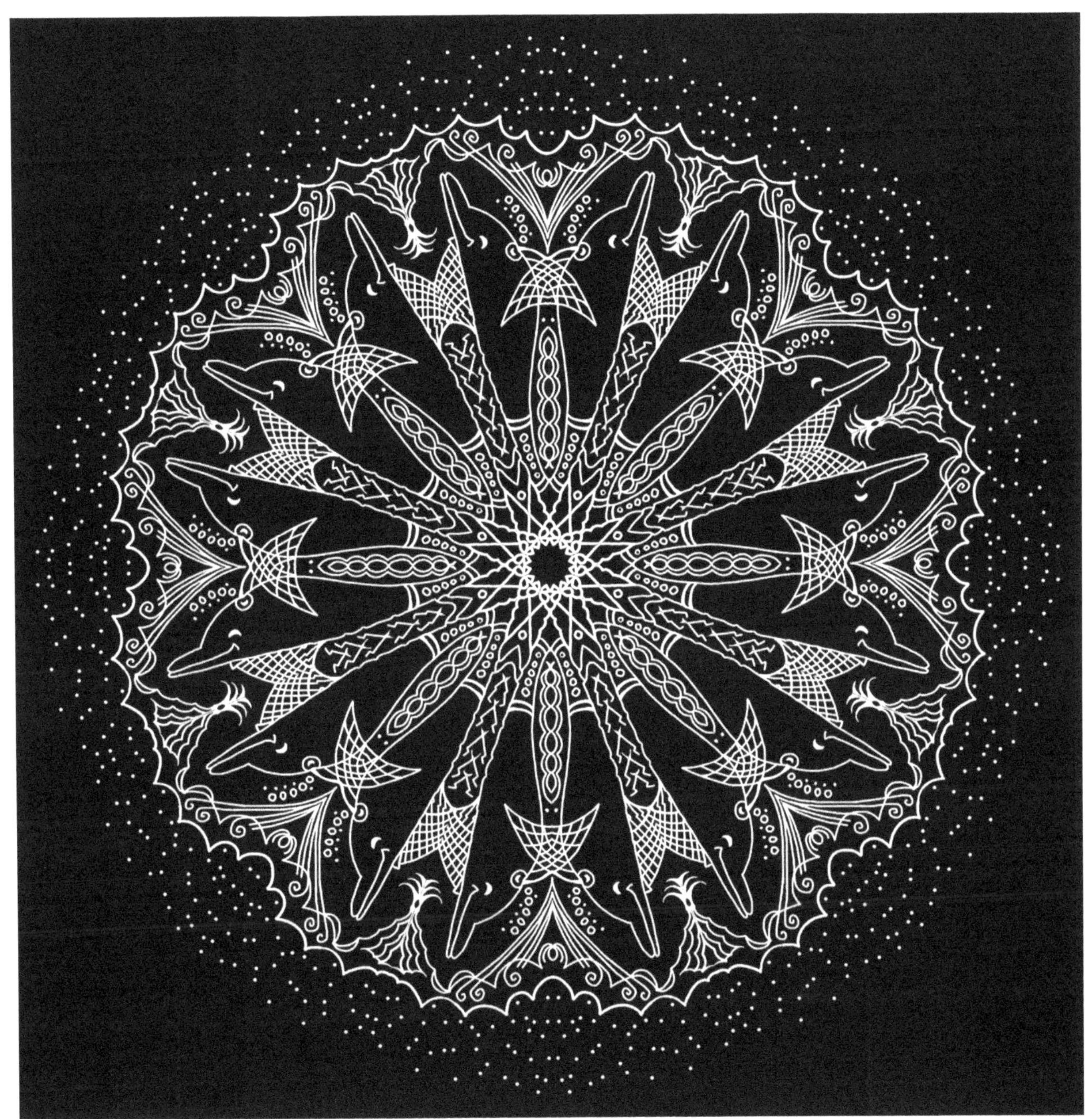

Dolphins Delight at Sunset

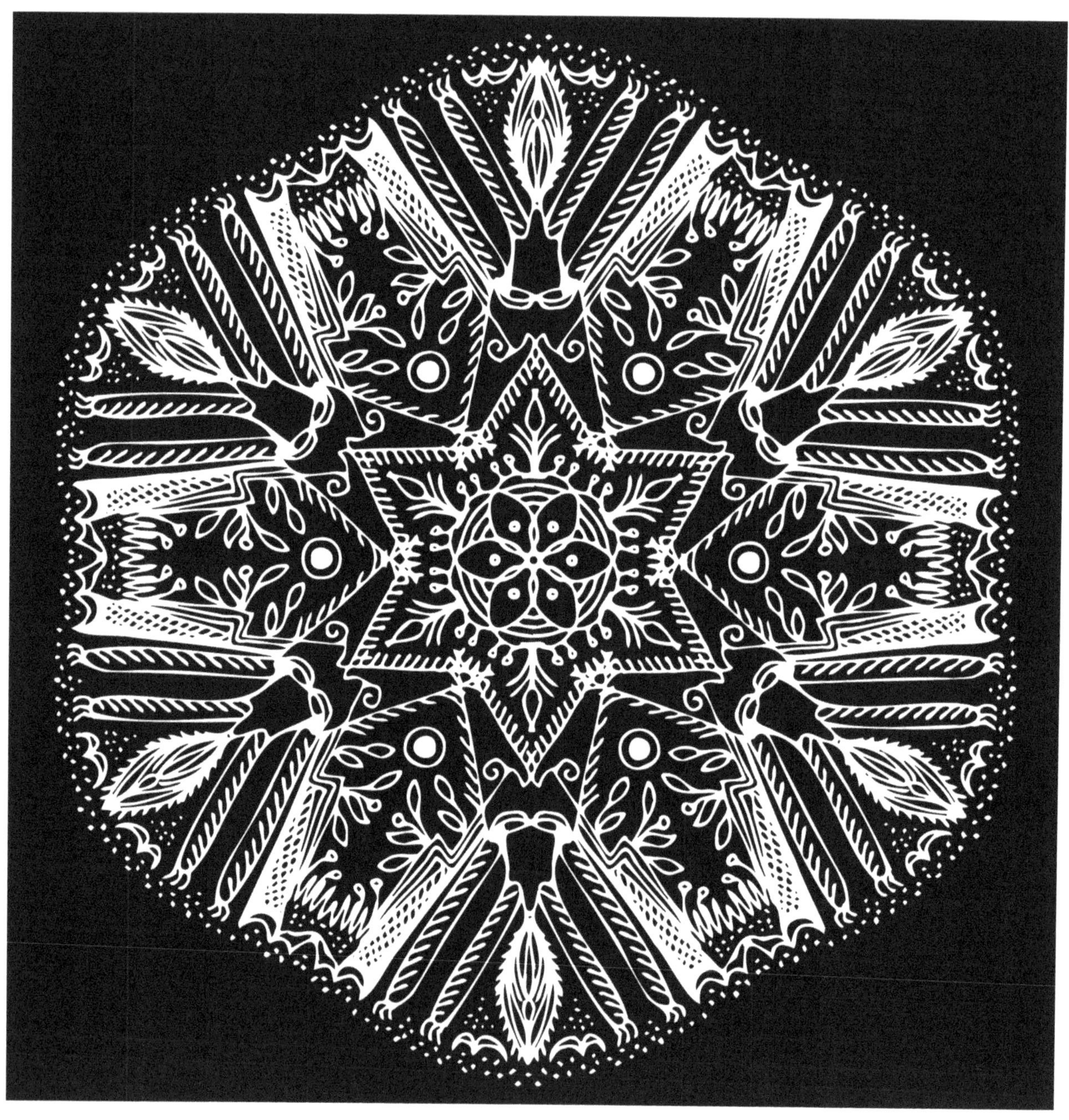

Is Cave Wolf Getting Ready to Come Out and Howl at the Moon?

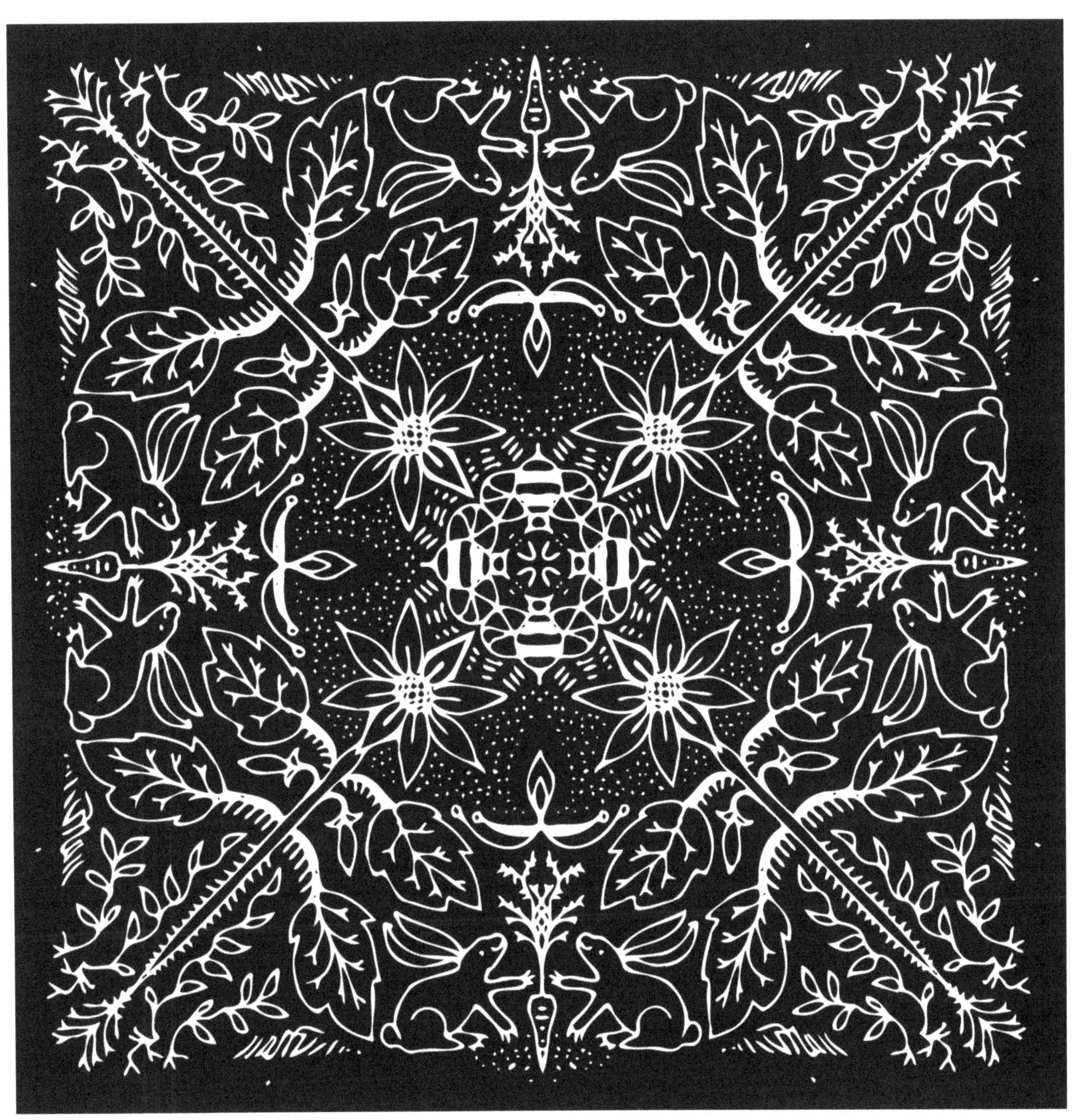

Bees, Carrots and Bunnies

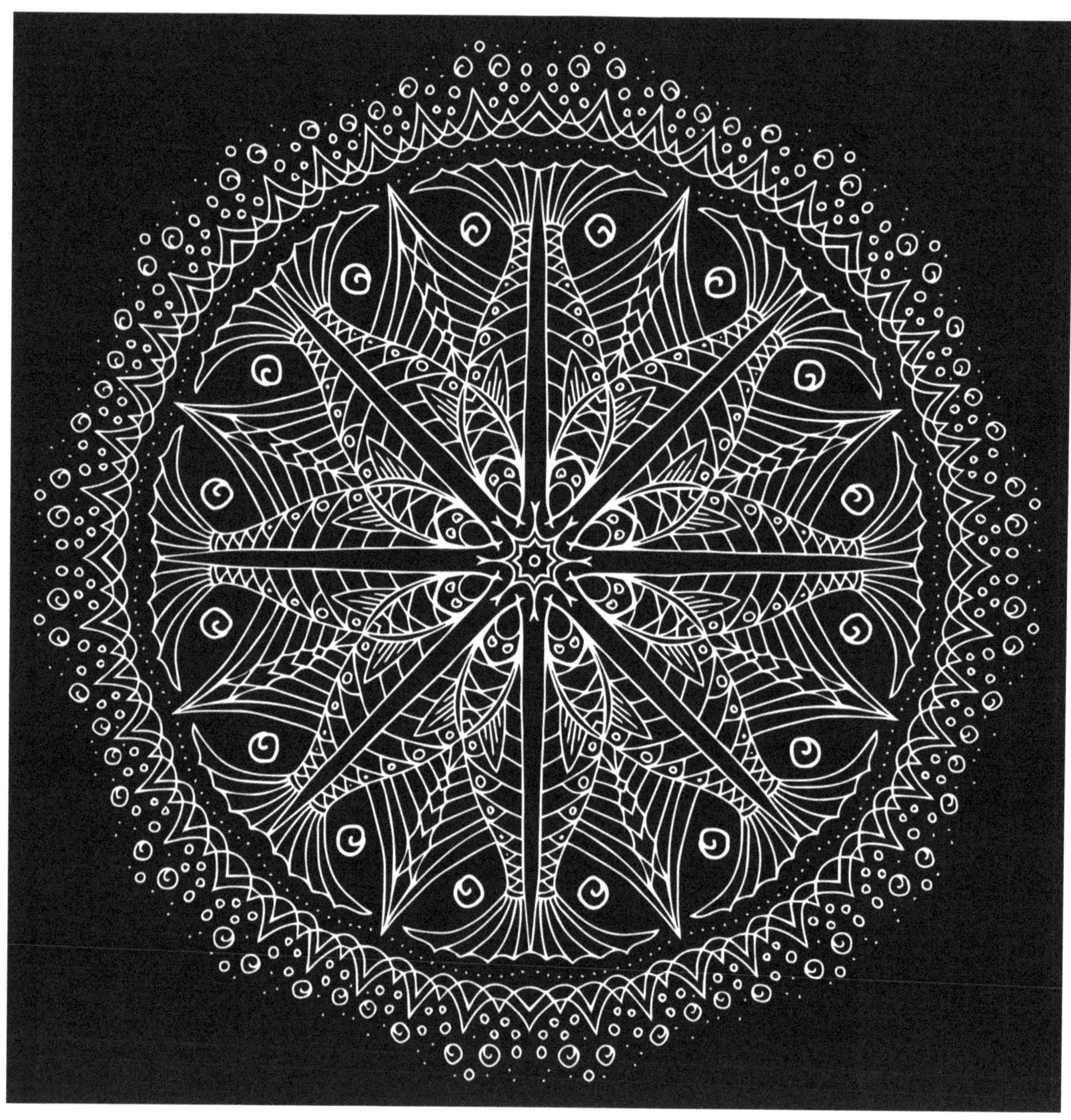

Fishie Vortex

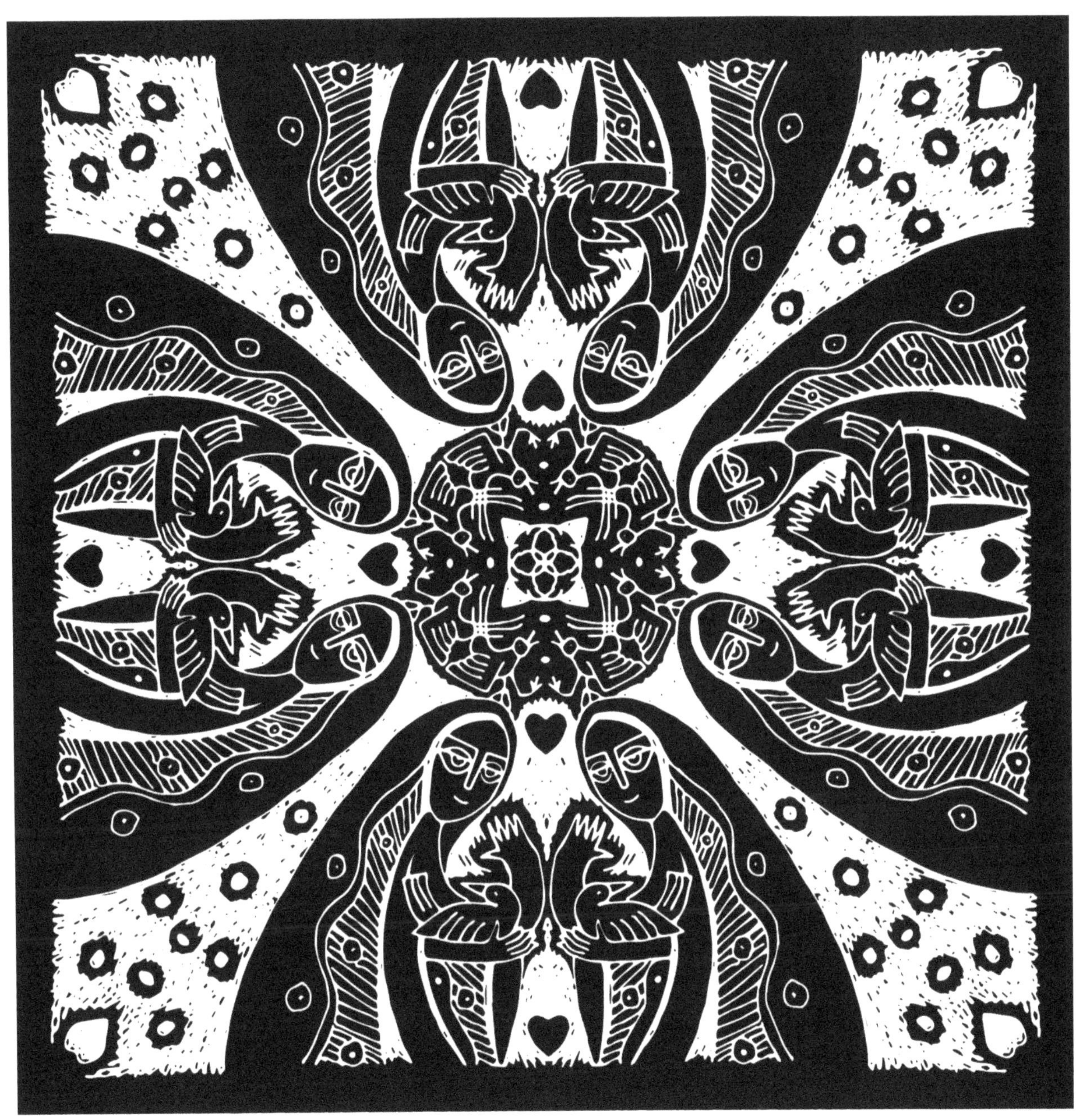

She Saved Poor Raven when His Wing Got Broken

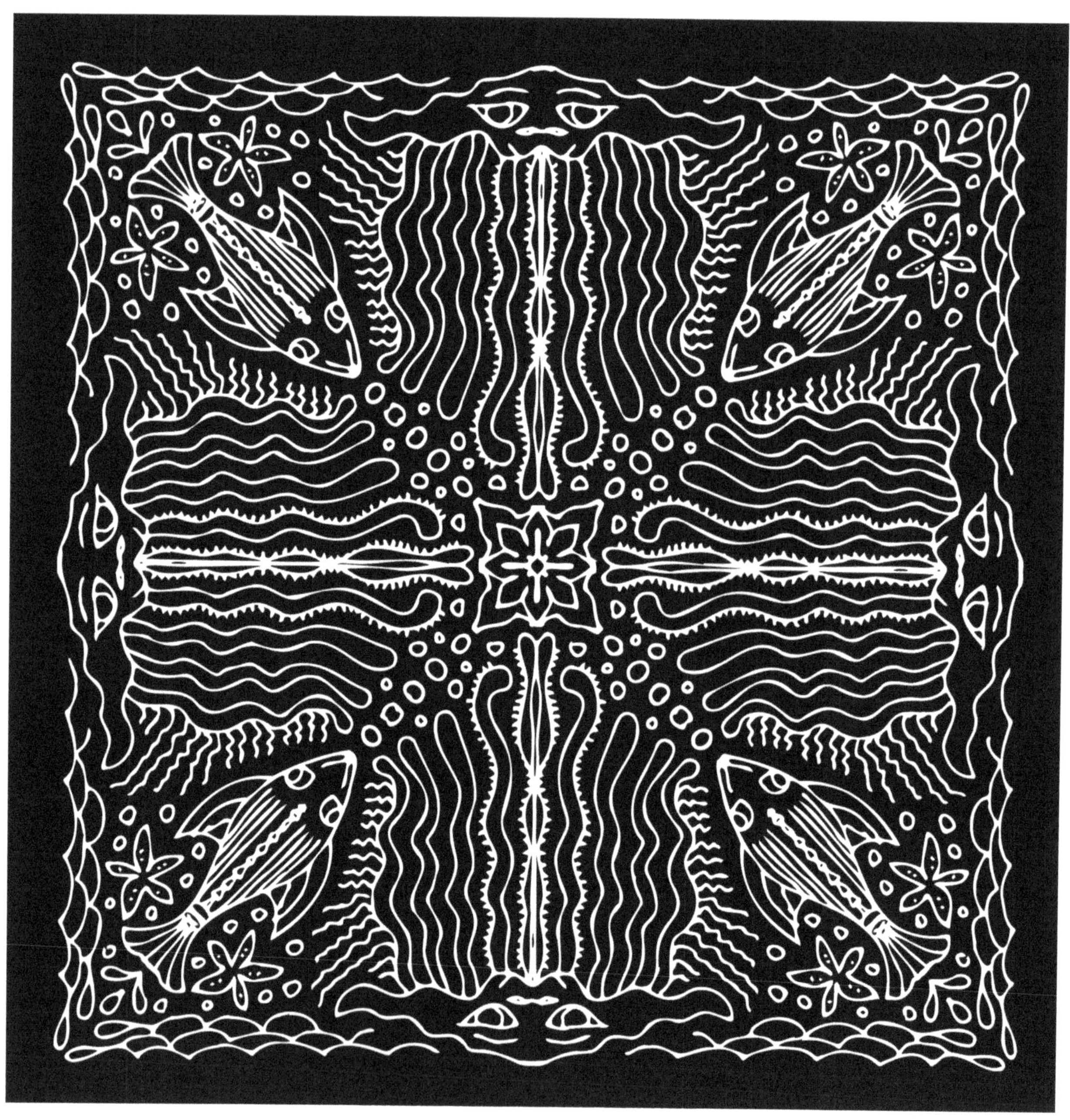

Sneaky Jellyfish Try to Hide

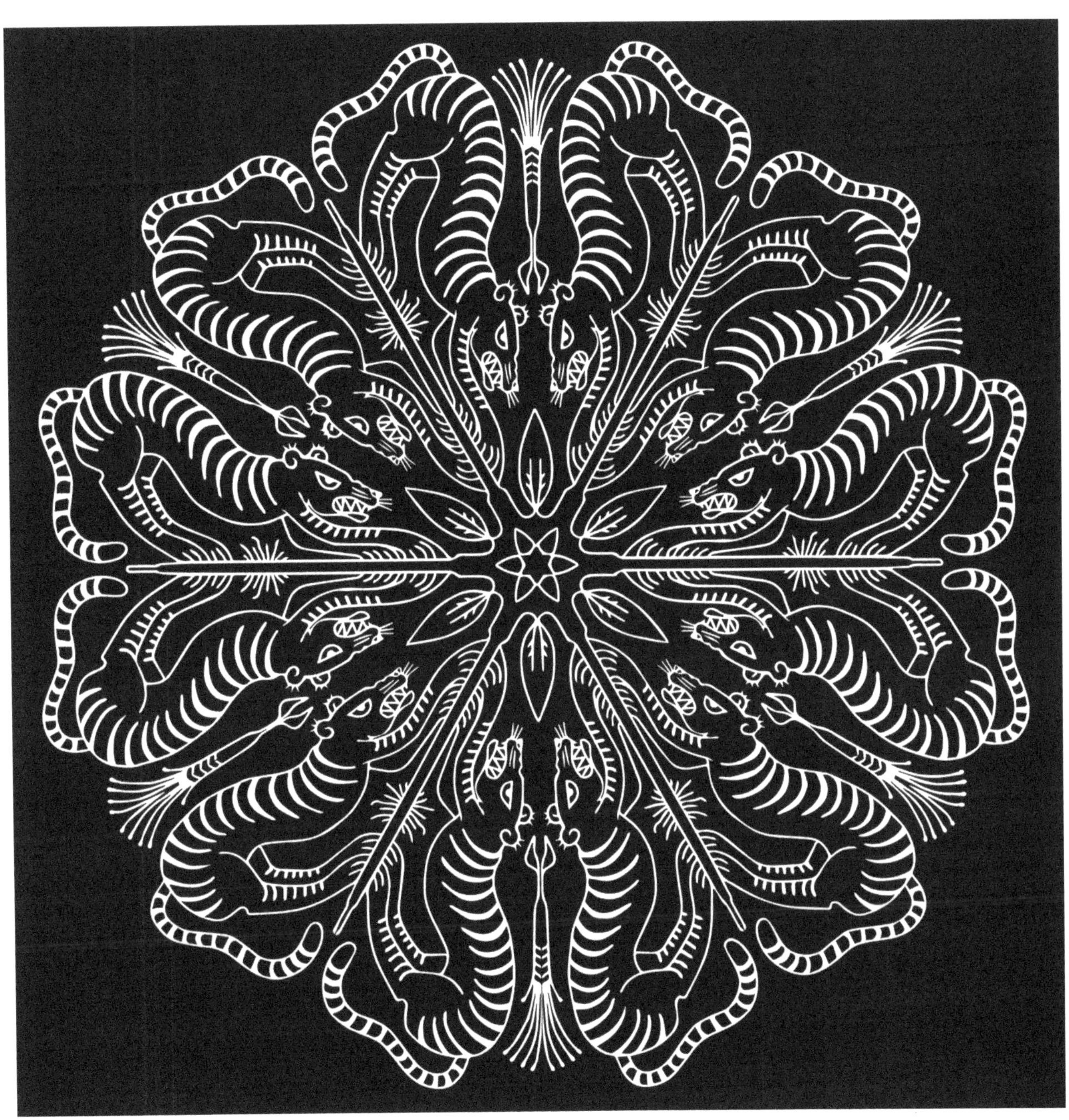

Fierce Tiger!

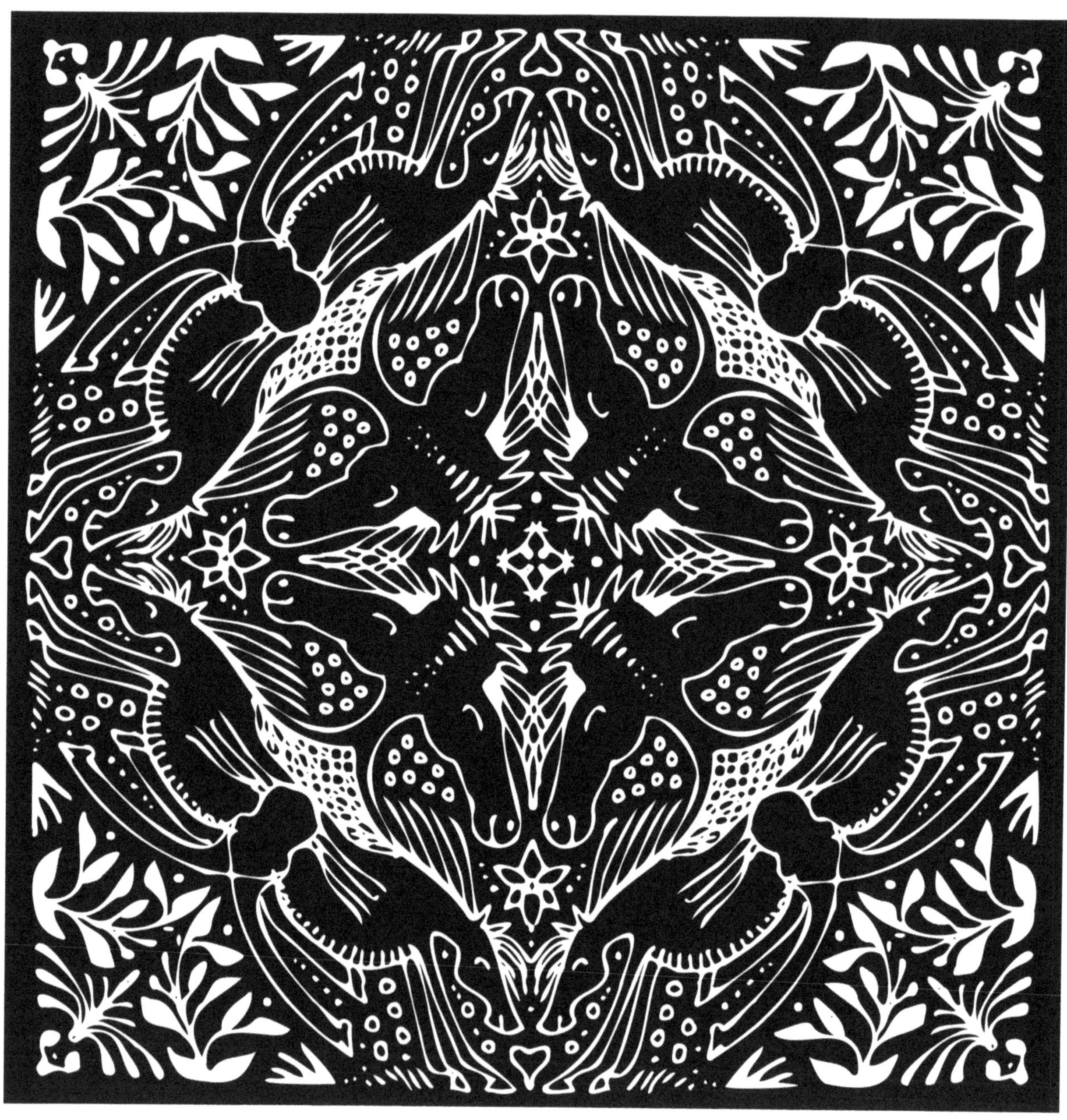

Freedom Means Kicking and Running Out in the Field

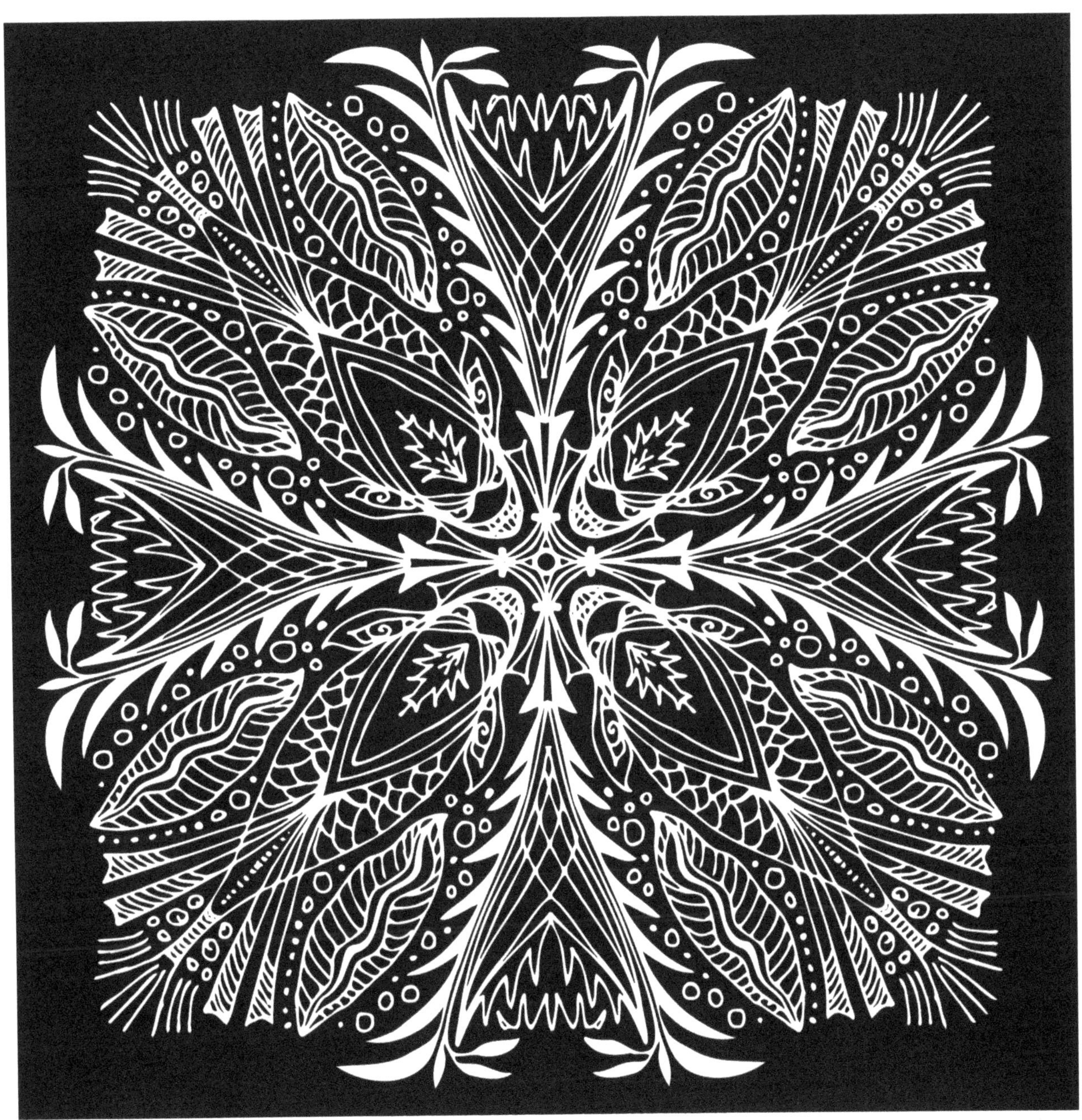

The Koi and the Giant Clam

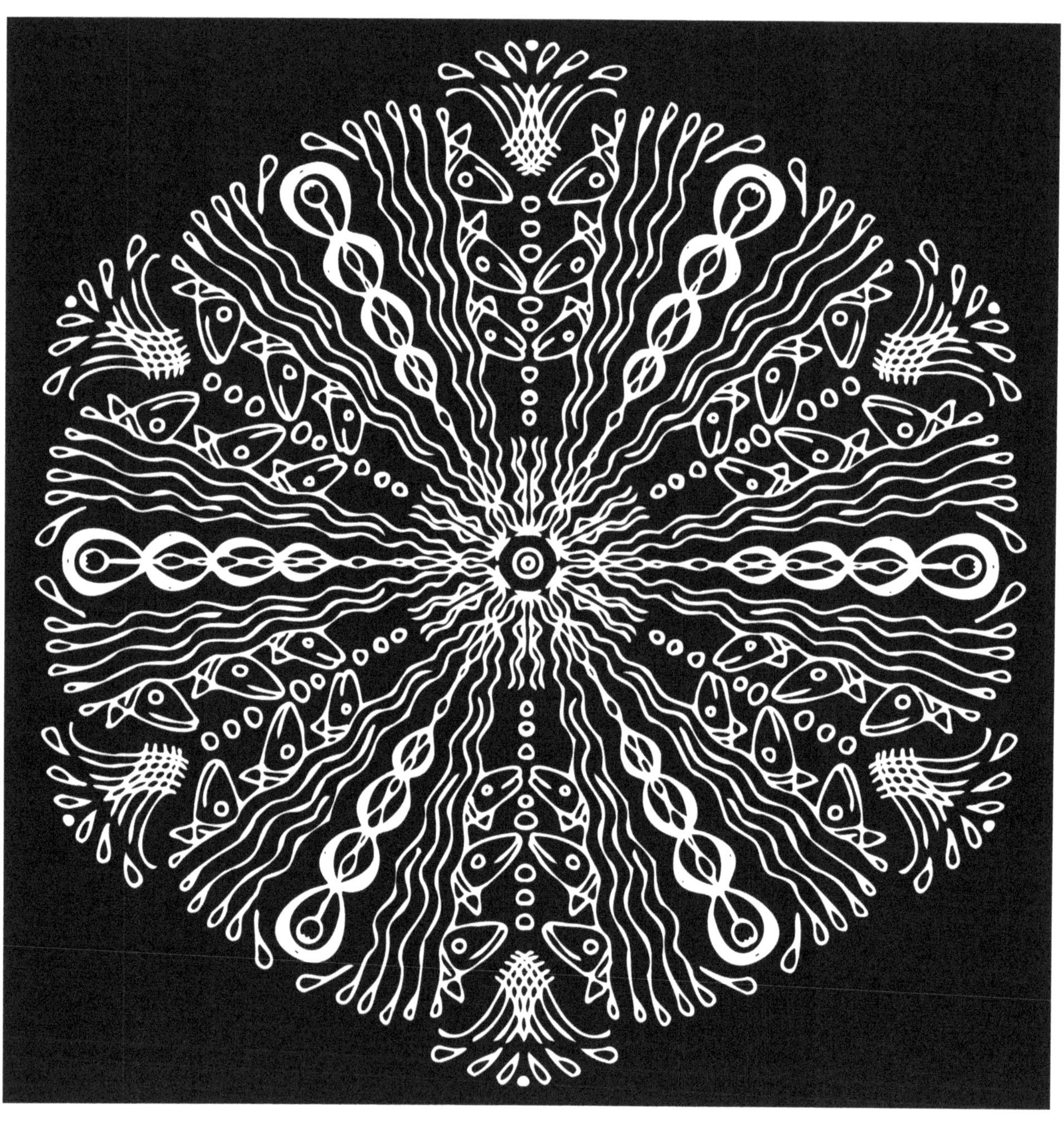

Come On Out of the Seaweed and Swim to the Moon

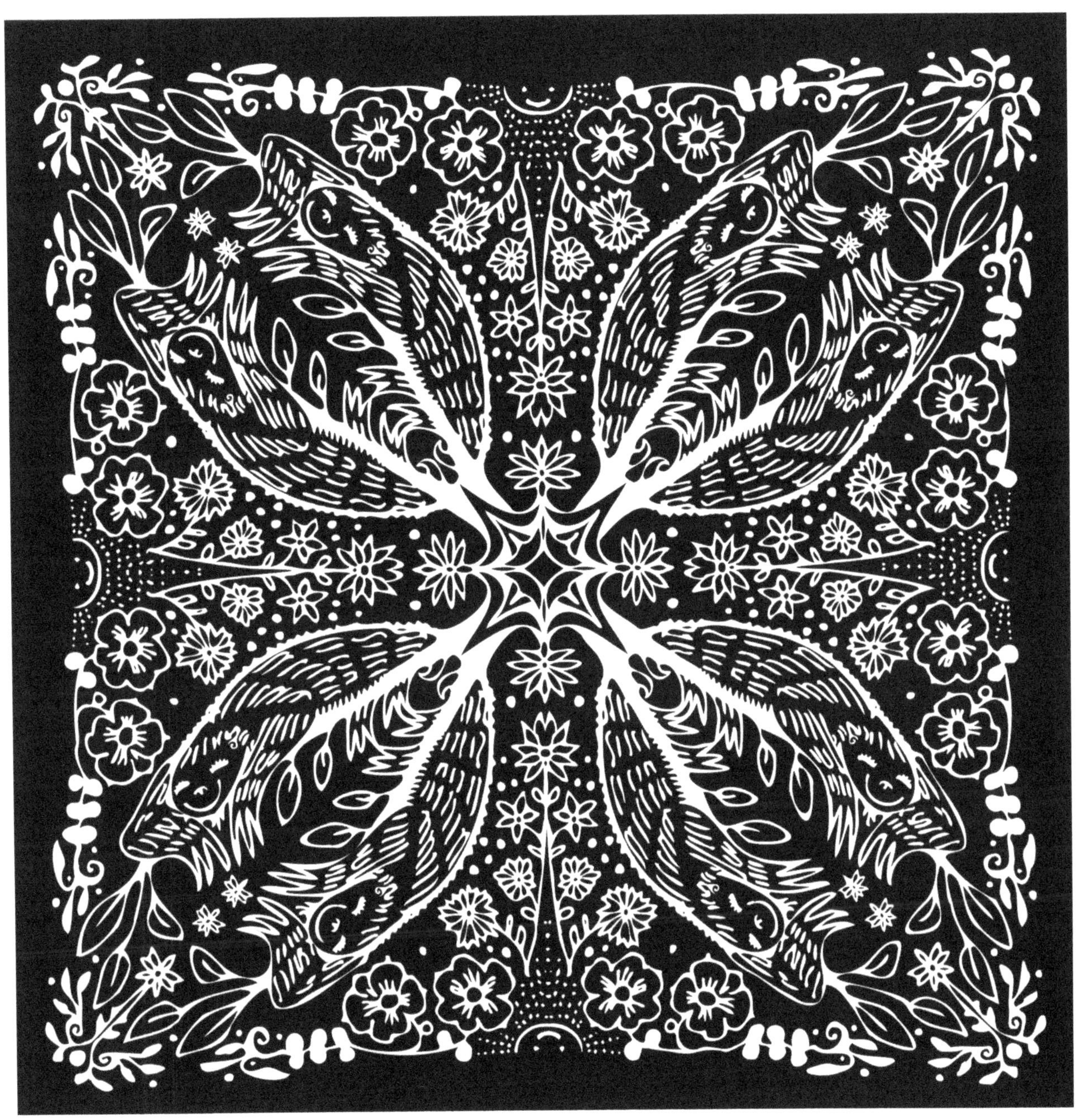

Lazy Sloth Loves His Garden

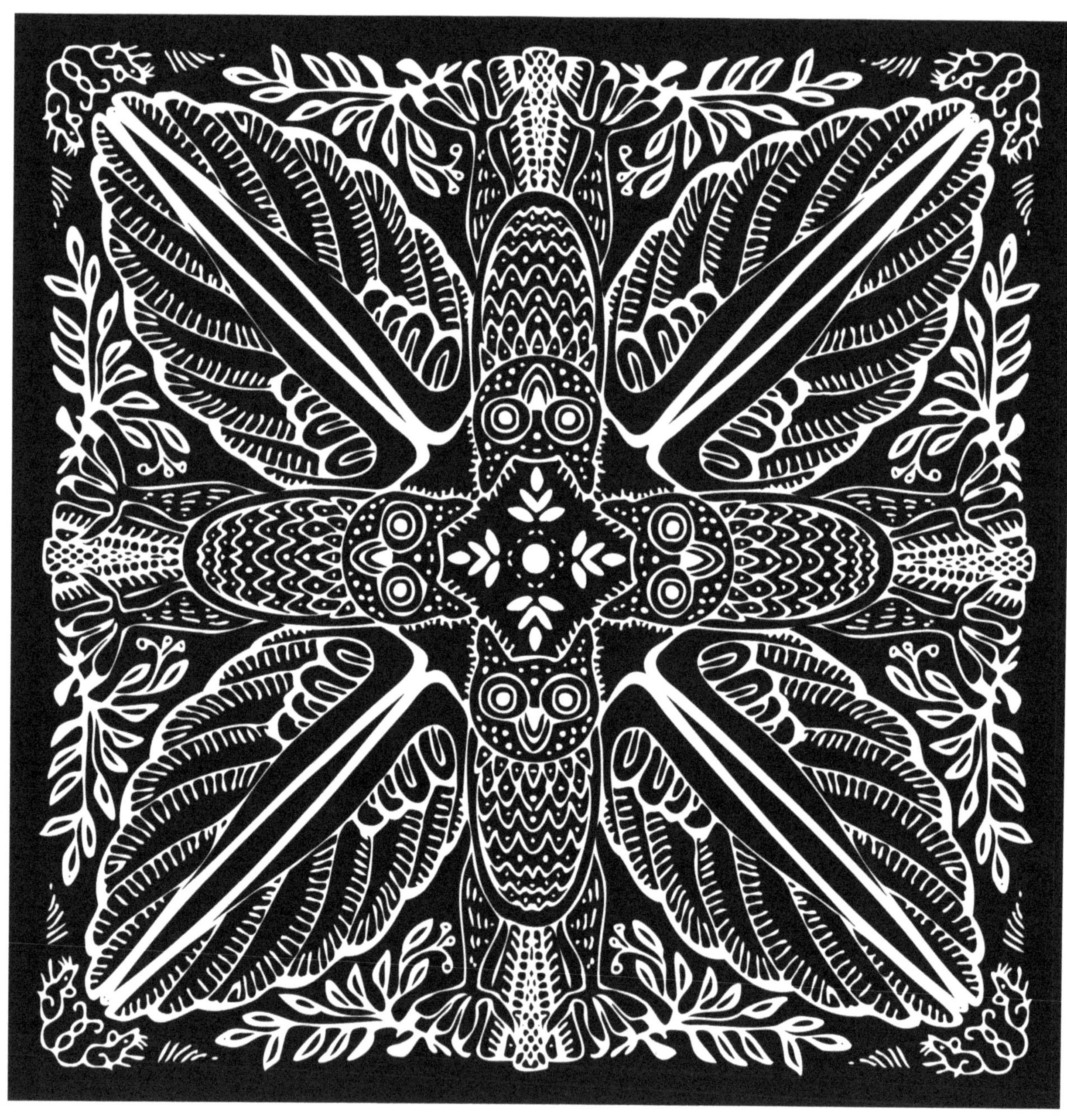

Night Owl Hoots Until Dawn

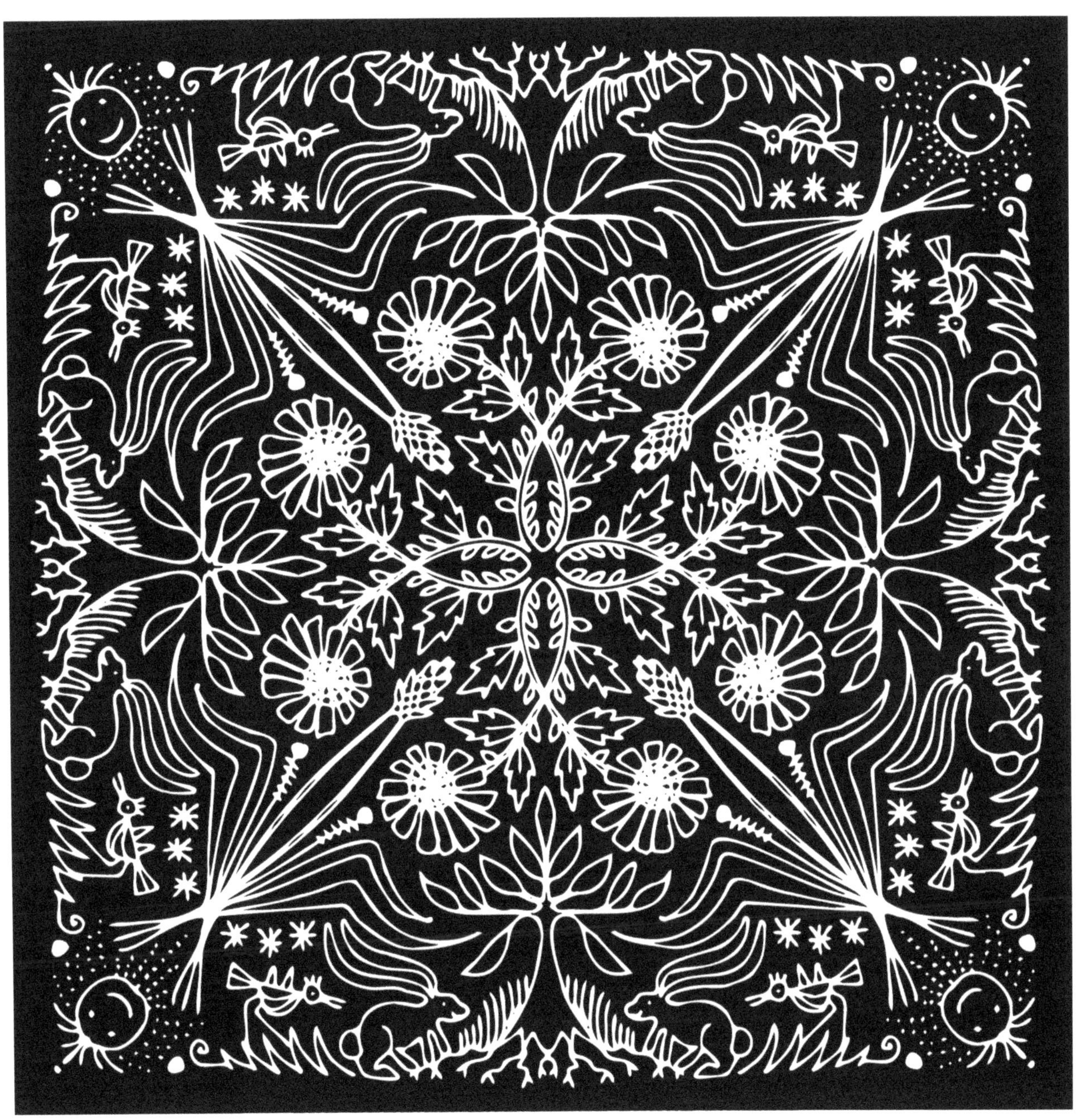

Sun Bunnies, Birdies and Sunny Flowers

Thank you!

I hope you've had fun going through these images!

My good friend, a doctor, told me she thought I was bringing mirth back to the world. I like that idea. Seems like it's needed in a big way right now. There will be more - I can pretty much guarantee that! So stay tuned....

I hope you get as much enjoyment out of these drawings as I have! If you'd like to license any of the designs, or purchase prints or products, please see the next page.

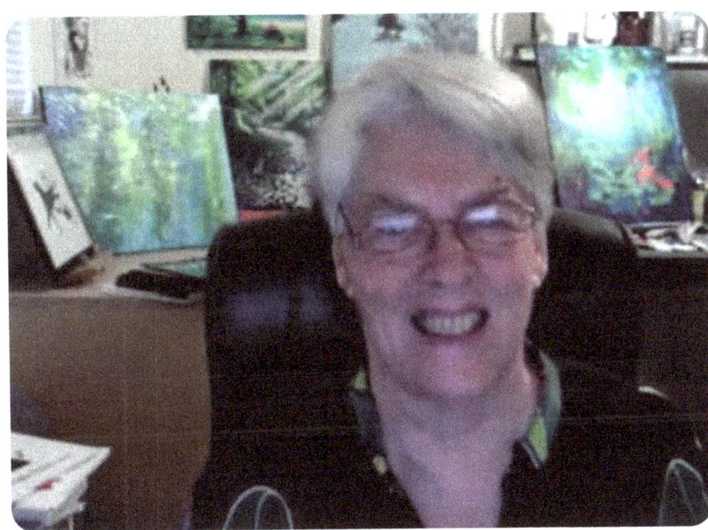

Much aloha -

Angela

Angela Treat Lyon
Chico, California 2021

Where to find Angela's work

The Unexpected Stories:
UnexpectedStoryArt.com

Paintings, sculpture, drawings, watercolors:
AngelaTreatLyonART.com

Most recent paintings, sculpture, drawings, watercolors:
LyonPaintings.com

instagram.com/angela.treat.lyon/

facebook.com/AngelaTreatLyon

Clothing, accessories, and other products:
Redbubble.com/people/AngelaTreatLyon

Books by Angela:
Amazon.com and AngelaTreatLyonBOOKS.com

Contact Angela:
530-809-7900 in California (Pacific time zone)
Lyon@AngelaTreatLyon.com

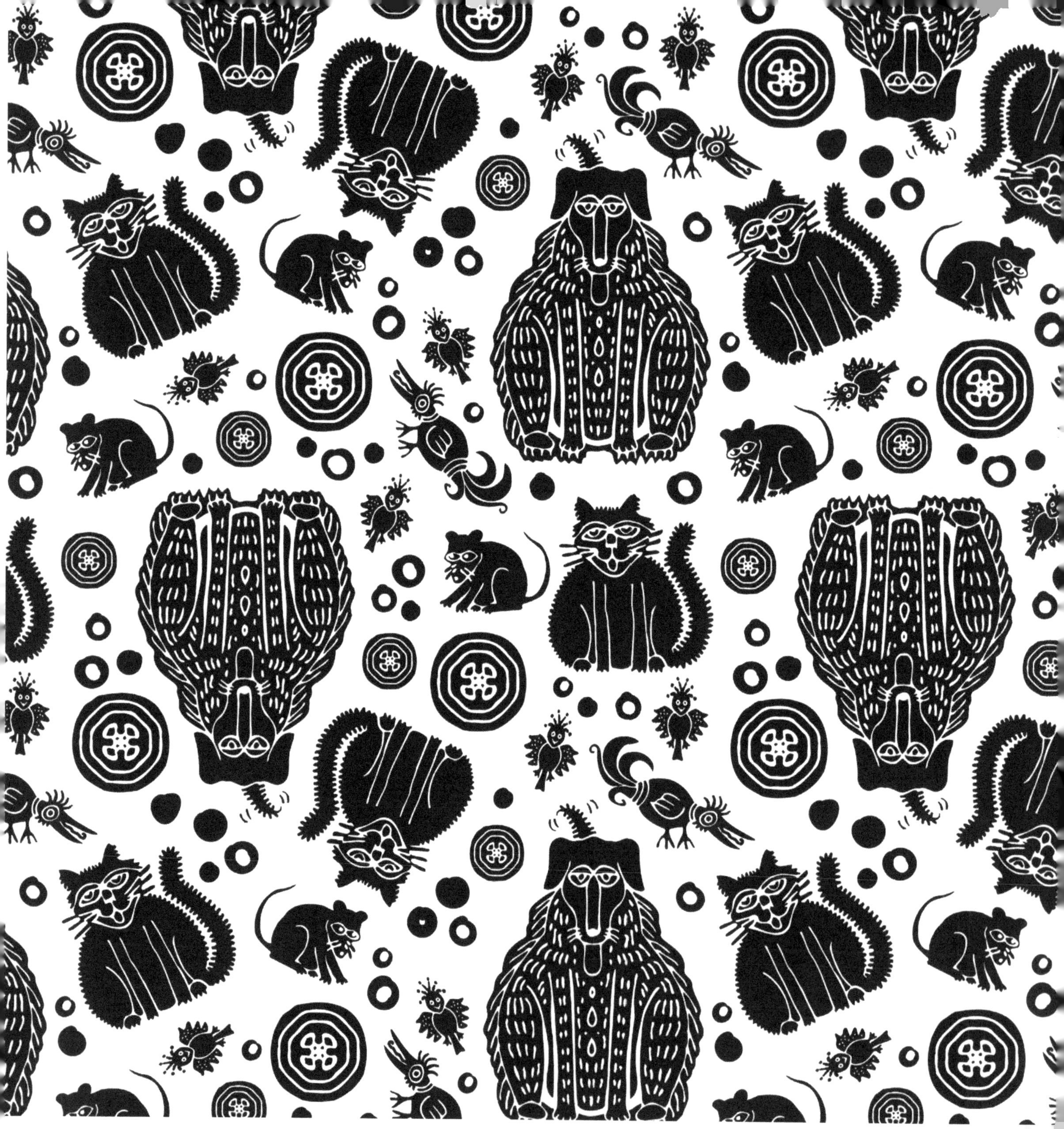

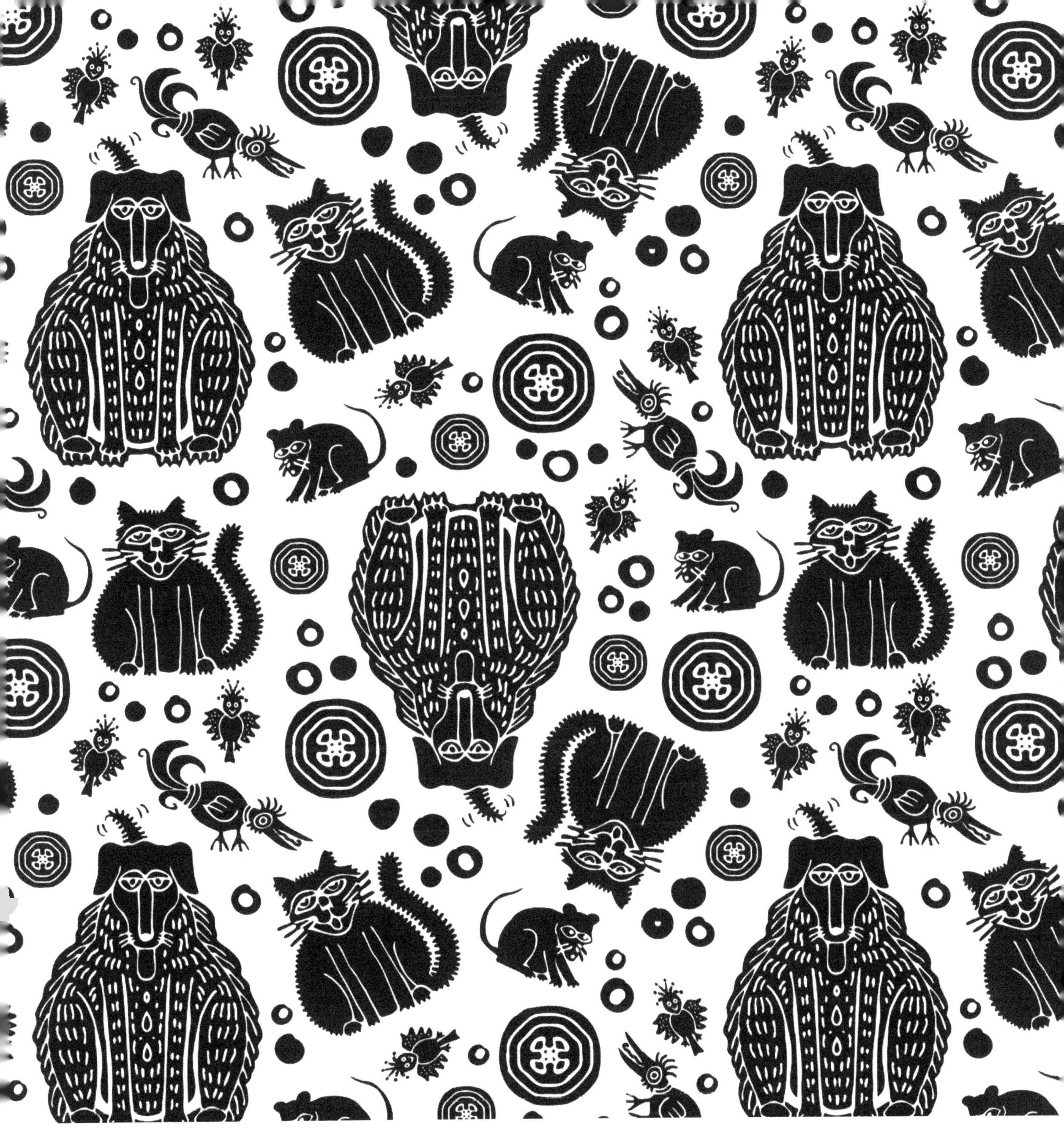

www.ingramcontent.com/pod-product-compliance
Ingram Content Group UK Ltd.
Pitfield, Milton Keynes, MK11 3LW, UK
UKHW061951290726
14090UKWH00021B/1174